PUFFIN BOOKS

TALES FOR THE TE

Once upon a time and long ago, in Ireland the art of story-telling was loved and practised by every man, woman and child. Wonderful tales of heroism and strife, giants and princesses, ancient magic and high deeds were retold again and again and loved by each new generation.

*Tales for the Telling* is a magnificent collection of these ancient fables and fairy stories, in which the legendary heroes and ogres rub shoulders with a few extraordinary and colourful mortals. Edna O'Brien has used her deep-rooted Irishness, and her exceptional talent as a story-teller, to capture all the vitality and charm of the ancient legends and stories. The result is a delightful retelling of the classic tales which will charm a new audience of children and adults alike.

Edna O'Brien is a well-known author of novels, short stories and screenplays. She grew up in a small country town in the west of Ireland and her feelings for that country and its people have coloured much of her writing. *Tales for the Telling* is her first book published in Puffin.

Michael Foreman has written and illustrated many books for children and has won awards from all over the world. He has illustrated three other Puffins in this series of tales from around the world: *Fairy Tales* and *The Saga of Erik the Viking* by Terry Jones, and *Seasons of Splendour* by Madhur Jaffrey.

# EDNA O'BRIEN

# *Tales for the Telling*

## Irish Folk and Fairy Stories

*Illustrated by*

## MICHAEL FOREMAN

PUFFIN BOOKS

PUFFIN BOOKS

Published by the Penguin Group
Penguin Books Ltd, 27 Wrights Lane, London W8 5TZ, England
Penguin Books USA Inc., 375 Hudson Street, New York, New York 10014, USA
Penguin Books Australia Ltd, Ringwood, Victoria, Australia
Penguin Books Canada Ltd, 10 Alcorn Avenue, Toronto, Ontario, Canada M4V 3B2
Penguin Books (NZ) Ltd, 182–190 Wairau Road, Auckland 10, New Zealand

Penguin Books Ltd, Registered Offices: Harmondsworth, Middlesex, England

First published in the USA by Atheneum Publishers,
a subsidiary of Macmillan, Inc 1986
First published in Great Britain by Pavilion Books Limited
in association with Michael Joseph Limited 1986
Published in Puffin Books 1988
This edition with black and white illustrations published 1992
1 3 5 7 9 10 8 6 4 2

Printed in England by Clays Ltd, St Ives plc
Set in 12/14 pt Lasercomp Photina

# *Contents*

# *Prologue*

Plaze your honours, boy-childs and dawters, wake up. Now when a lot of paiple are in the shlapes, dhraming, you can make a bogthrot and parsaive a moighty carouse of little paiple, discoorsing and cod-acting an' workin' their mettyfisics. They are from the other worruld and are very impident and shpake diffirint tongues altogether. The place you'll find them is out av the highways because they likes to thravel in furpaths and they're always to be found in forts and raths. They can make your heart sthand still wit the deeds they do be doing and the shee music that they makes. They rayports have it that some of their thribe are made up of avil spirits, avil fairies, avil divils and the Pookha. He's a quare fella. He's a horse and not a horse, a bhlack fella wit eyes of fire, breathin' flames a blue, wid a shmell o' sulphur an' a shnort like tunder an' a tail twisting and laceratin'. Now while he's doing wan thing the fairies do be dancin' by the light of the moon an' witches wid shnakes on their arrums and eyes of dead men like aurnaments in their hair do be rhiding on sthicks an' bats an' owls, up to their dhirty thricks and laughin' until they nearly sphlit. They shtop wather in a spring, inconvanience paiple, dhry the cow's milk or make her kick the pail, set the thatch on fire or spile the crame in the churn or bewitch the butter, an' be razon of their devilment desaive paiple or put them undher an inchantment. But they can do no harrum to anyone that fares God, barren they're not drunk and they can do no harrum to them that do pinnance an' say their prayers at night. You'll parsaive them on certain nights afther the moon is up and most paiples shound ashlape. They are very ontoxicated and they will try immijetly to get you to join in their fun and go to France but don't go or you'll be ruinated. Be as perlite as anything, sthand your ground an' don't get into any mularkin'. . . .

## Two Giants

Finn was the biggest and the bravest giant in all of Ireland. His deeds were known far and wide, lions lay down before him, his chariot flashed like a comet through the fields of battle, and with his 'Venomous' Sword he lay low a hundred men while with the other hand casting his sling at a troop of deer or a herd of wild boar. Along with that he had a thumb of knowledge and when he sucked his thumb he could tell what was happening anywhere in Ireland and he could foretell the future encounters. Now when Finn was no longer young, the rumour went about that there was a giant in Scotland who was Finn's equal and his name was McConigle. McConigle was not only fierce in battle, but when he walked up a hill the earth trembled under his feet, the trees wobbled, and the wild game fled to their lairs. By one blow of his fist he flattened a thunderbolt one day, turned it into the shape of a pancake and kept it in his pocket as a souvenir. He too had a way of prophecising by putting his middle finger into his mouth and sucking on it. Now the two giants had never met but it was reported that McConigle intended to come over to Ireland, to fight Finn and to give him a pasting.

It so happened that one day Finn and his men were away from home and were busy making a bridge across the Giant's Causeway. In the distance they could see a messenger galloping towards them and Finn wondered if his wife Oonagh had taken sick or if there had been some breach in their fortifications at home. The messenger announced that Finn was to come home at once and then whispered something in Finn's ear that made him tremble with rage.

'So he's on my trail,' said Finn as he stood up and with that he pulled up a big fir tree, banged the clay off it and with his knife snedded it into a walking stick, so that it was both a walking stick and an umbrella. To see Finn walk was like seeing a mountain move and in no time he was across one county and heading towards home. He was going up a slope when in the mud he saw footmarks which were as big as his own. In fact they were the exact shape as his own and Finn thought 'Lo' and had his first feeling of terror and doubt. Never before had he come across a giant the length and breadth of whose feet were as enormous as his own. He widened his chest and let out an almighty roar just to make his presence felt and it echoed all over the valley and was heard by his wife in her own home.

Finn's palace was on the top of a hill called Knockmany and it looked out on another mountain called

Culamore and there was a deep gorge in between.
Finn had settled here so that he could see his enemies
a long way off and as well as that he could throw the
bodies of his prey into the gorge for the crows to
fatten themselves on.

'Oh my bilberry,' said Finn as he saw his wife
Oonagh who had plaited her hair and put on a silk
dress to please him. At once Finn asked if the reason
she had sent for him was true.

''Tis true, Avick,' said Oonagh and went on to tell
him how McConigle had pitched tent at the far side of
the province and had his famous thunderbolt in the
shape of a pancake in his pocket, and called himself
The Invincible. Finn put his thumb into his mouth to
verify all these things and found that they were true.
He could only use his gift of prophecy on very trying
and solemn occasions such as this was.

'Finn darling, don't bite your thumb,' said Oonagh
very sweetly as she led him into the house where
there was a dinner prepared. Finn squatted at one end
of the low table, Oonagh at the other and along with
maidens to wait on them there were harpists playing
in order to soothe Finn. He started by having sixteen
duck eggs, eight pig's crubeens and three raw onions
for his digestion. The main course was a haunch of
roast venison and it was so long that it stretched
between them down the length of the table, a sizzling
roast dotted with berries and all sorts of herbs. But no
matter how much he ate or drank there was a frown
on Finn's forehead and a big brown ridge like a furrow
on the bridge of his nose because of his thinking.

'Dearest,' said Oonagh as she bobbed along and

began to stroke his great naked back. Finn always removed his cloak before he sat down to eat.

'You'll best him, you always do,' said Oonagh, but Finn shook his head and said it was perilous because according to this thumb he and McConigle had equal amounts of strength, ate the same amount of food, weighed the same, and were equally matched in daring, wisdom and cunning.

'What else does it say?' Oonagh asked and Finn put his thumb right inside his mouth and shut his eyes in order to concentrate.

'Take care you don't draw blood,' said Oonagh.

'He's coming,' said Finn, 'he's below in Dungannon,' and at that he jumped up.

'When will he be here?' said Oonagh.

'He'll be here before long,' said Finn and he began to put his vest and his jacket on. He looked at his wife and for the first time she saw fear and apprehension in his eyes. She decided that she would have to help him and make use of her own enchantments. Oonagh was in with the fairies too and with her wand had once turned a hussy into a hound. She told Finn that she would help him to succeed.

'How, how?' said Finn, hitting the table and sending delph in all directions.

Oonagh hurried out of the doorway in order to give a message to her sister who lived on the opposite mountain at Culamore.

'Grania,' said Oonagh, 'are you at home?'

'I'm in the kitchen garden,' said Grania, 'I'm picking berries for a tart.'

'Run up to the top of the hill and look about you

and tell us if you see anything untoward,' said Oonagh. They waited for a few minutes with Finn pacing up and down and servants fanning him with great leaves.

'I am there now,' said Grania.

'What do you see?' said Oonagh.

'Oh lawsie me,' exclaimed Grania, 'I see the biggest giant I've ever seen coming out of the town of Dungannon.'

'What is he like?' said Oonagh.

'He's something terrible to behold,' said Grania and went on to describe a giant of about twelve feet in height, his hair all the way down to his waist, his face ruddy like any giant's except that he had daubed blood over it and, most unnerving of all, his three eyes. He had an eye in the middle of his head that was rolling round like the hands of a clock. Not only was the ground shaking beneath him but the birds in the trees were dying of fright. Along with that he was laughing out loud as if he had just heard the most hilarious joke.

'He's coming up to leather Finn,' said Oonagh to her sister.

'Finn has my sympathy,' said Grania and then she just announced that the giant had picked up a white goat and was wringing its neck and was obviously going to eat it raw.

'I'll tell you what,' said Oonagh, 'call down to him and invite him up to your place for a bite to eat.'

'Why so?' said Finn, unable to follow his wife's drift of thought.

'Strategy,' said Oonagh, 'strategy.'

Grania called across to say she'd be glad to oblige and she'd entertain the monster but she was a bit short of bacon and of butter.

'I'll fling you some across,' said Oonagh and she snapped her fingers for a servant to bring a flitch of bacon and a firkin of butter. However, before throwing them she forgot to say her charms and didn't the butter and the bacon fall into a stream and get carried away.

'Never mind,' said Grania, 'I'll give him heather soup and I'll put shredded bark in it to give him indigestion.'

'Good on you,' said Oonagh and she winked at Finn.

'He'll skewer me,' said Finn.

'Don't be ridiculous,' said Oonagh, although to tell you the truth she could see a situation where she herself might be a dainty morsel, a little fritter for the giant's supper.

'My courage is leaving me, I'll be disgraced,' said Finn.

'Two heads are better than one,' said Oonagh as she went towards the place where she kept her magic threads. She drew nine woollen threads of different colours, she plaited them into three plaits, with three colours in each one; she put a plait on her right arm, another round her right ankle, a third round her heart, and in that way Oonagh was protected. Then she got going. She asked the servants to go up in the loft and bring down iron griddles and a child's cradle. She got them to make cakes but she hid the griddles inside the cakes and then baked them in the fire in

the usual way. When they were done she dusted
them over with flour so as to hide any protuberances
and she put them on the window to cool. Then she
put down a large pot of milk which she later made
into curds and whey and showed Finn how to pick up
a curd in his hand and make it smooth as a stone.
Then she got a nightgown and a shawl and dressed
Finn in it and put a nightcap on his head. She told
him that he would have to get into the cradle and
completely cover himself with clothes, with only his
two eyes peering out.

'I can't fit in a cradle,' said Finn.

'You'll have to double up,' said Oonagh.

16

'I'll have to triple up,' said Finn as she pushed him towards it.

'You must pass for your own child,' said Oonagh.

'But I'm not a child,' said Finn and he was afraid that he had taken the cowardice too far. Oonagh ignored his mutterings and just put him into the cradle and covered him up with great wool blankets and red deerskins.

'What do I do?' said Finn.

'Whist,' said Oonagh because they could hear the bruiser coming up the hill and giving a skelp of his axe to the dogs to shut them up. He strutted across the courtyard and when he arrived at their door he put a hand around either oak pillar and bellowed 'Anyone home?'

Oonagh came forward all shy and mincing and gave a little gasp to signify to him how formidable he was. He had rat skins and coon skins dangling from his ears and his third eye was rolling about like a spinning top.

'Mr McConigle,' said Oonagh.

'The great McConigle,' said the giant and then asked if he was in the house of Finn.

'Indeed you are,' said Oonagh and gestured towards a chair to make him welcome.

'You're Mrs Finn, I suppose,' said the giant.

'I am,' said she, 'and a proud wife at that.'

'Thinks he's the toughest giant in Ireland,' said Mc-Conigle.

'It's a proven fact,' said his wife proudly.

'There's a man within three feet of you that's very desirous of having a tussle with him,' said McConigle and he looked around in order to sniff out his rival.

'Is he hiding from me?' he asked.

'Hiding?' said Oonagh. 'He left here frothing, he's gone out to find you and it's lucky for you you didn't meet him, or you'd be a dead man now, your head on his pike as an ornament.'

'You vixen,' said McConigle and he roared with rage but Oonagh was in no way dismayed.

'He's twice your height and much better built,' said she.

'You don't know my strength,' said McConigle.

'In that case would you turn the house,' said Oonagh.

The giant stood up, put his middle finger in his mouth, thought for an instant, then went out, put his arms around the house, picked it up and put it facing a different way. Finn in his cradle was now facing in a different direction and there was sweat pouring out of him with heat and nerves.

'You're a handy giant,' said Oonagh and then told him that she was short of water, but that there was a fine spring under some rocks and that if he could split the rocks she'd be most obliged. He took his axe out from under his leather apron, struck at the rocks and tore a cleft that was hundreds of feet deep. Oonagh began to have doubts.

'Come in and eat,' said she and added that although her husband would make mince of him, the laws of hospitality must be observed.

She placed before him six cakes of the bread and a mound of newly churned butter and she sat down pretending to be polite. He put one of the cakes in his mouth, took a bite and let out the most terrible growl.

'What kind of bread is this?' he said fiercely.

'Fresh bread,' said Oonagh, cool as a breeze.

'And here are two teeth of mine gone,' said he as he hauled out two big molars that were grey in colour and shaped like drinking horns.

'Why,' said Oonagh, 'that's Finn's bread, the only bread that he eats, him and the child there.' At that she offered another cake. As soon as he put it in his mouth another great crack was heard and he let out a yell far fiercer than the first, so that the baby mewled. 'Thunder and giblets,' said he as he pulled out two more teeth with bits of gum on them.

'Well, Mr McConigle,' said Oonagh, 'if you can't manage the bread, don't bother with it but don't be disturbing my child.'

'Mammy, mammy, can I have some bread?' said the baby from the cradle and its voice gave McConigle a start. Oonagh very cleverly handed a cake that had no griddle in and McConigle was flabbergasted as he watched the child gobble it up.

'I'd like to take a glimpse at that lad in the cradle,' said he.

'Certainly,' said Oonagh and she told the little baby to get up and prove himself the worthy child of his father. Now the baby stood up, looked at McConigle and said, 'Are you as strong as me?'

'Thundering giblets,' said McConigle, 'how dare you insult me.'

'Can you squeeze water out of a stone?' said the child, and he put a stone into McConigle's hand. McConigle squeezed and squeezed but not a drop of liquid came out.

'Watch me,' said the child and he put his hands

under the covers, took out one of the white curds that looked exactly like a stone and squeezed until the liquid came out in a little shower from his hands.

'My daddy is training me,' said he, 'but I have a lot to learn yet.'

McConigle was speechless.

'I'll go back to sleep now,' said the child, 'but I'd hate to waste my time on anyone that hasn't my daddy's strength, that can't eat daddy's bread or squeeze water out of a stone.' Then he slipped down and as Oonagh was pulling the covers up over him he raised his index finger and gave a word of warning to McConigle. 'I'd be off out of here if I were you as it's in flummery my father will have you.'

'What he says is a fact,' said Oonagh as she tucked Finn into the cradle and patted him to let him know how proud she was.

'I'm thinking it is,' said McConigle.

'You're not in his league at all,' said Oonagh and went on to remind McConigle that if the child was that strong he could only guess at the immensity of the father.

'Will you let me feel the teeth of that infant?' said he still in a quandary.

'By all means,' said Oonagh and she took his hand and she stuck it straight into Finn's mouth explaining that the child's best teeth were in the back of his head. McConigle was amazed to find a baby with a full set of grinders and more amazed when he felt something snap and then felt his finger detach itself and when he pulled out his hand there was a big wound where his finger of knowledge had been. Finn had eaten it. So shocked was he and so horror-stricken that he fell down. Finn rose from the cradle and laid roundly on the monster with his bare hands. He could easily have killed him with his sword but that McConigle begged for his life and Finn being a chivalrous hero gave it to him. After that McConigle made his peace, picked up his teeth and his accoutrements and promised to go home to Scotland and never set foot in Ireland again.

## The Leprehaun

Bridget was sent out as usual to fetch a bucket of water but when she got to the well near the house she found it had dried up so she had to go across some fields to another well that was near an old disused monastery. Now as she was walking along she suddenly heard tap tap, tap tap, and she stopped and thought to herself 'could it be', because Bridget like every other girl knew that the little fairy cobbler came up from underground and mended shoes. But not only that, but that the leprehaun had the power of bestowing wealth on anyone who caught him and who kept him in their sight.

Leprehaun – Leithe Brogan, or Fairy Shoemaker

'Oh,' said Bridget to herself, 'this is my chance to be a rich woman.'

So she put the bucket down and she went in near the hedge and she crept along until she caught sight of him. Quite a beau he was in his red coat laced with gold and cocked hat with a green feather, an apron over his knees and he hammering away at a little silver dance shoe. Beside him was a little vessel full of drink. So up she came behind him and she seized hold of the back of his coat with the command, 'Deliver or die.'

'Oh moidy,' says he in a squeaky voice, 'a highwayman.'

'Wirra man,' said Bridget, 'I'm just a young girl.'

'You're hurting me,' said the leprehaun and he tried to wriggle out but of course she had a tight hold of him and informed him that she had no intention of letting him go until he told her where the crock of gold was hidden.

'I don't know,' he whimpered.

'You sly boots,' said Bridget and she squeezed harder.

'Such a purty colleen ketchin' a body as if he was a robber.'

'If you don't tell me I'll cut the head off you,' said Bridget.

'What wrong did I do to be thrated like this?'

'No wrong yet,' said Bridget, enquiring what was in the vessel.

'Beer,' said the leprehaun, 'strong beer.'

'Did you steal it from a house?' said Bridget.

thrated – treated

'I brewed it,' said he and boasted that he learnt brewing off a Dane.

'In that case, you know where the crock of gold is,' she said. 'You're a smart sprite.'

'I'm a poor cobbler,' he protested.

Bridget threatened to carry him into the village and to plonk him down on the big weighing scales in the market place where the entire town would see him and where he would first be cross-examined and then squeezed like a sausage by stronger men than her.

'I'm bested, I'm bested,' he said.

'You are,' said Bridget. 'So you might as well get down to business.'

'Who'd think it, a nice girl like you,' said he.

'Give over your plamais,' said Bridget, 'and bring me to where the loot is.'

'We have a bit of a walk,' said he. Then he asked to be let down. But Bridget was taking no chances; she picked him up in her arms and she carried him like a baby.

'It's demasculating,' he said, kicking and yelping, but Bridget gave him a few clouts and threatened to dump him in the well if he didn't behave himself.

They crossed a field and climbed over a gate, then into a paddock, past the lime kiln and over a ditch into a huge field that was covered in ragwort. It stretched from one end to another, great high stalks of yellow ragwort.

bested – beaten
plamais – sweet talk

'Let me down,' said the leprehaun.

Bridget let him down but made sure to keep a good hold on him in case he disappeared. They began to wade their way into the middle of the field and every so often he put his ear to the root of a stalk to 'reconnoitre' as he put it.

'It's under here,' said the leprehaun, 'dig there and you'll get your guineas.'

'Dig!' Bridget exclaimed in a huff. She had expected to pull the stalks up and find the booty – she was not in the mood for digging.

'You'll have to dig deep,' said the leprehaun, 'ten feet or maybe more.'

'With what? My hands!'

'With a spade,' said the leprehaun, a bit saucily.

Bridget wanted him to accompany her back to the farm to get the spade but he convinced her that that was a mistake. He said that he had to keep an eye on the stalk in case another leprehaun came, because they were avaricious, like humans, and they were bound to be passing by as day began, and they betook themselves to the burrows and chambers that led to their secret abodes.

'They wouldn't trick *you*,' she said.

'Oh, they would, they're all thieves,' he said.

'Suppose you do a disappearing act,' cautioned Bridget.

'I'll tell you what,' said the leprehaun, 'I'll put a garter around it and you'll recognise it even if I'm not here.'

'Right,' said Bridget.

He slipped off a tiny little red garter that was

26

keeping up his wool sock and hung it over the piece of ragwort.

Bridget ran for dear life. She crossed the fields, she passed the ruin, she took the stepping stones over the stream and went directly to the farmyard where shovels and implements were kept.

Back she was, panting but delighted at her speed. However, a nasty shock was in store for her: what did she see but a red garter on every single stalk of ragwort and no sign of Mr Slimy Leprehaun.

'Oh thunder and sparables,' she cried and she started to dig. Well, she dug and she dug and she dug and all she found was clay with worms and maggots in it, and she swore by the vestments that if ever she caught that bucko she'd squeeze him into putty, but she never did find him and the chances are she never will.

## The Fool

There was a king in the western part of Ireland and he had a son that was called Amada. Amada's mother died and the king married again but the stepmother didn't like the son and she never gave him anything tasty to eat. She fed him just on meal and water, and nettles. However, he did grow up to be strong and the stepmother was afraid that he would harm her own children so she asked her husband, the king, to send him away. The king agreed to send him away but Amada refused to go until his father would give him a sword that was so sharp it would cut a fleck of wool falling on it. The king knew a famous blacksmith, who was in debt to him, and he asked him to make a sword that had no equal in the land and they called this sword the 'Invincible'.

Now he travelled for many days and many nights and eventually he came to a castle and when he went in he found no people there, but a great feast spread out on a table, so he sat down and he tucked in. When he had finished the dinner in staggered three princes, gashed and wounded.

One of them struck a bit of the wall of the castle with a flint and at that moment the whole castle looked as if it was on fire. So Amada sprang up and said, 'What do you think you're doing putting a castle on fire?'

'Oh, Amada,' said one of them, 'don't say that to us for we are nearly killed as it is. The castle is not on fire, it's a ruse. Every day we have to go out and fight three giants, Big Slat, Medium Slat, and Little Slat. We fight them all day long and just as night is falling we kill them, yet they always come to life again and are as ferocious as ever by morning. If they didn't see this castle lit up they would come here and murder us while we slept.'

Hearing this Amada was filled with a longing to fight and he promised the princes that he would do his best to defend them.

They set out the next morning and they travelled to the glen where they met the three giants. Amada told the princes to take on Medium Slat and Little Slat and that he'd tackle Big Slat himself. Big Slat strode towards him and took a furious buffet at his face but Amada dodged him and held his sword crosswise and challenged him to a battle. They made the hard ground into soft and the soft ground into spring wells and they made rocks into pebbles and pebbles into gravel and the gravel fell all over their heads like hailstones and the birds of the air came to witness the fight and so did the beasts of the forest. In the end Amada split the giant open from the mouth to the tail and the two halves of him fell apart like two pieces of timber. Then he went to the rescue of the princes and very soon the other two giants were on the ground as dead and as mute as their leader.

Amada told the princes to go on home and that he would sit by the corpses and observe if they came to life again. However, he was so exhausted from his fierce fight that he fell asleep, and as he slept a very old hag in a grey wool mantle appeared. Her mouth was twisted to one side and she had a green tooth. She also had a goose feather and a jar of ointment and straightway she began to brush the ointment on to the giants' wounds. The giants were up and eating bowls of porridge when Amada wakened.

'You dirty bog trotting profligate,' said Little Slat as Amada stood up.

'You tattered Demalion,' said Medium Slat and they set on him with spades, pitchforks, scythes and a flail. Their fight took them lurching and punching across the province and when Little Slat met his gory end Medium Slat cried out, 'I thank God for the chance of killing you,' and he hewed and he hacked until poor Amada was gashed from head to toe but in the end Amada got the better of him.

'You have killed my brothers, it will cost you your life,' said Big Slat who had been pursuing him across the hills. They fell into grips and they made the hard ground into soft ground and the soft ground into spring wells and they made rocks into pebbles and pebbles into gravel and the gravel fell over their heads like hailstones and the birds of the air came to witness the fight and so did the beasts of the earth. At last Amada ran his sword a forearm's length through the giant's temple and knocked him senseless to the ground.

This time the giant was doomed because it was only at a precise moment in the thick of night that the hag could bring them back to life, and by now it was near morning. In revenge the hag put Amada under a bond. It was this: he would lose the power of his feet, his sight and his memory if he did not go and fight the Black Bull of the Black Wood. Having said this she disappeared but she left behind the feather and the jar of ointment. Amada began to brush his wounds with the ointment and soon he was fresh and unblemished again. So he buckled on his sword and he started off to fulfil his obligation to meet the Black Bull of the Black Wood.

He travelled that day and that night, and next day as night was falling again he came to a little hut in the middle of a wood, its roof covered with wings of many coloured birds and a yew tree beside it. There was a red-haired woman standing in the doorway.

'Come in,' she said, 'you will have neither loss nor hurt in my house.'

In he went and he told her about his series of fights and about the bond the hag had put him under. She said there was one thing that could be a protection against the bull and she went and fetched it. It was a cloak. Then she explained what he had to do.

'Throw it over the rock, hide behind the rock and

when the bull comes tearing forward he will dash at the red cloak and will crash against the rock and stun himself. Then you are to jump on his back and with that sword of yours fight for your life. If you win the fight I will be glad to welcome you back.'

Amada went to the spot. He saw the bull tearing towards him, he spread the cloak over the rock, hid behind it and with the fury of his thrust the bull split the rock and stunned himself. Amada lost no time, jumped on the bull's back and with his sword again hacked and hewed and yet the bull tossed him and threw him off. A horrible fight ensued. They made the hard ground into soft and the soft ground into spring wells and they made rocks into pebbles and pebbles into gravel and the gravel fell over their heads like hailstones and the birds of the air came to witness the fight and so did the beasts of the forest. After a long time Amada ran his sword a forearm's length through the bull's neck and the bull's head fell off and he died letting out the death groan. But as he was dying the severed head spoke and put Amada under a bond and it was to fight the White Stag of the Hill of the Waterfall.

Amada healed his wounds with the ointment, went back to the little hut and told the red-haired woman that he was now under an obligation to fight the White Stag of the Hill of the Waterfall.

'Oh,' she said, 'I'm sorry for you because no one has ever met the White Stag and come back alive.' She gave him food and drink and in the morning she directed him to the waterfall. She said the sword was never made that could go through the White Stag's

hide except for one place – above his heart was a tiny little lozenge-shaped spot and if the sword could pierce there the stag would be killed.

Amada went to the appointed spot and saw the stag bounding towards him in a bellicose mood.

'What are you doing here?' asked the stag.

'With this sword I have killed Big Slat, Medium Slat and the Black Bull of the Black Wood,' said Amada.

The stag scoffed, threw a mound of earth in the air in disdain, then lifted Amada up on his horns and swung him around so viciously that Amada saw the four corners of the field and the far ends of the sky in one terrible spin and was certain that he would end up in the next world. However, the stag swung him back to earth again and tossed him into the next field, presuming him dead. But the stag was rash in thinking that. Amada lay there, put a little ointment on his wounds and soon he was able to get up and face his assailant. The stag was drinking at a brook and Amada had the advantage of coming on him from behind.

'Oh rash stag,' he called out and the stag turned and they fenced, the one using his sword, the other his slate-coloured horns. They made the hard ground into soft and the soft ground into spring wells and they made rocks into pebbles and pebbles into gravel and the gravel fell over the country like hail and the birds of the air came to witness and so did the beasts of the earth. After a long and wizard struggle Amada had the stag pinioned against a wall and when he saw the lozenge-shaped spot he struck at it and drove his sword the length of a forearm

34

through the stag's heart. As the stag was dying he put Amada under a bond to fight the Emissary of the King of Transylvania.

Amada healed his wounds, went back to the hut and told the red-haired woman of his next obligation. She explained how the tall spectre from Transylvania would appear in the sky, and would land in a sphere of cloud and stand up with the whole world between his legs. She said, 'If ever he's fatigued he goes up in the sky in his Chairoplane cloud and stays there until he is refreshed. You can let him go up once but if you let him up a second time he will vanquish you when he comes down – that is his strategy.'

As the woman gave him the most lavish supper of all Amada feared that his next opponent was worse than all the others, having the strength of a beast and the cunning of a man. He didn't sleep a wink all night and next morning he set out with a pounding heart. The clouds parted and the Emissary of the King of Transylvania soared down and stood with the whole world between his legs.

'You yalla squid,' he said as he spotted Amada.

Amada told him that he had killed Big Slat, Medium Slat, the Black Bull of the Black Wood, the White Stag of the Waterfall and that now he had come to kill the Emissary of the King of Transylvania.

'I give you a choice,' said the Emissary, 'do you want to die by my squashing you with my hand or by my sword?'

'I am a knight and if I have to die I'd rather die by the sword,' said Amada.

So they both drew their swords.

The clashes could be heard hundreds of miles away. Every second they sprang at each other and every other second they each drew back free and scatheless. Their garments were rent, their shields half gashed and at one point they plunged into a bog hole with the Emissary shouting 'Your end is nigh.'

However, he sank several feet and while he was trying to rescue himself Amada crawled out of the bog hole, all black and smeared and leapt over the beds of turf until he came to a lake. The lake was surrounded by rushes and he hid among them and as he did he saw the Emissary coming towards him and he saw a mist gathering around the Emissary and he realised that he was going up in the sky as foretold. Remembering the words of the red-headed woman he did not lose heart; he took a big gout of air and jumped into the sky as limber as a shuttlecock. He got above the Emissary's head, drew his sword and struck the Emissary and killed him dead.

The last words of the Emissary were that Amada had to fight the Silver Cat of the Glen.

Amada rubbed his wounds and went on back to the little hut where the red-haired woman was surprised to see him. He told her that his next adversary was the Silver Cat of the Glen.

'Well,' said she, 'this time I have to say that I think it's hopeless because that cat has powers that are not of this earth.'

She gave him his supper and put him to bed and in the morning she told him the one thing that might help him but added that it was a slender chance. The cat had a weak spot inside the stomach and she said it was probably impossible to get to and was as small as a grain of pepper.

'I am very afraid that we will not meet again,' she said and this time she kissed him goodbye.

Amada went to the cliffs above the sea and looked down and there under a huge precipice he saw that there was a cave with a horseshoe over it and it was in this cave the cat lived. Amada let himself down by rope and waited. When it was midday the cat came out to sun herself. Seeing Amada she let out a hiss that actually stopped the tide and she asked him how he had the impudence to come to her lair.

'I have killed Big Slat, Medium Slat, Little Slat, the Black Bull of the Black Wood, the White Stag of the Waterfall and the Emissary of the King of Transylvania, and before night I will have killed the Silver Cat of the Glen.'

'You will be in shreds,' she said and she sprang. He raised his sword and he struck out and they both fell to a great vicious fight and they made the hard ground into soft and the soft into spring wells and the rocks into pebbles and pebbles into gravel and the gravel fell above their heads like hailstones and the birds of the air came to watch and so did the wild beasts of the forest and the seals came out of the sea and the fishes popped up and the whole of nature was stunned by the massacre.

Now the red-haired woman was watching at the well in her garden and she became very worried because she had predicted to Amada that if there was a sight of honey uppermost in the well, then it meant he was winning, but if there was a sight of blood uppermost in the well then the cat was winning. What was happening was that one minute the honey was uppermost and the next minute the blood was uppermost and so she knew that it was touch and go. At length the blood and the honey got mixed in together and she cried out in grief because she knew that it augured badly. What she feared was true, for when the fight had gone on a long time the cat used the great ivory nail which was on the end of her tail and with it tore Amada open from the crown of his head. As she tore him open and he was about to collapse she opened her mouth with glee; at that moment he stuck the sword down her gullet and got to the little black spot on her stomach and they died at the same instant.

Now it was not long before the red-haired woman arrived at the place and she found Amada and the cat on the seashore with the surf rolling over them. She was very sorry for poor Amada but suddenly she remembered about the ointment and she took it from his pocket and rubbed him carefully with the feather. Slowly he began to stir, then he opened his eyes and then he smiled and she helped him up.

They set out along the shore and they walked through the glen and over many lonely valleys until they got back to the castle of the three princes who had been living happily since the giants had been killed. With them was their beautiful sister and the moment Amada saw her his blood and his pace quick-ened.

'I must leave you now my son,' said the red-haired woman.

'Stay,' said Amada.

'I was only sent to serve you in the trials of battle . . .
you are in love now and in love each one travels alone.'

With that she disappeared and as Amada walked
through the great door he realised that he was more
frightened than he had been before meeting any of his
adversaries and that for the first time he was under
the enchantment of love.

## The Magic Apples

A poor man called Marty lived in a little hut in the middle of a rushy field and every morning and every evening he was seen, on his knees, traversing the field, gathering something. Now what he gathered was manna which fell to the earth with the dew and sufficed him for his breakfast and his supper.

One day a beggar man came to the hut, along with his daughter, Sinead, and he asked for food and shelter. Marty shared his manna with them and after the supper they went to sleep beside the fire. In the morning when they were about to leave Marty realised that he had taken a fancy to Sinead so he called the beggar man aside and asked if he could have her as his wife.

'How will you support her?' asked the beggar man.

'On manna,' said Marty, 'the way I support myself.'

The beggar man hummed and hawed until Sinead showed by her smile that she was prepared to stay and become Marty's wife. She was tired of travelling, tired of walking barefoot over roads and by-roads and

40

she hated knocking on doors begging for bread and milk.

The couple were married and in time they had one son whom they named Marteen after his father. They lived on the manna and they never felt hungry because of it being so peculiarly filling. After some years Marty died and so the wife had to gather the manna herself. She was a lazy woman and she didn't like going out into the fields twice a day so what she decided to do was to bring out a big basin and to gather enough manna for a week. But her greed and her laziness were her undoing because after that not a bit of manna fell on the field and she was so hungry that she had to go and work for farmers and on Sunday she had to beg at the chapel gates. Now her son Marteen was a very precocious boy: he could do tricks with matches, he could make fire with pieces of stone and he was great at somersaults. He had it in mind to travel the world when he grew up. He used to sit at crossroads and talk to pedlars and enquire of the big deeds that went on in the big world.

One day a pedlar told him about a lord in the city of Limerick who had a beautiful house in its own grounds, who kept a capital table, served fine wines and victuals, had his carriage and equipage and a daughter that had no equal for sauciness. Marteen decided that he wanted to see this lord and this daughter and that he would go there and impress them with his clever ways.

'You fool,' his mother said and reminded him that he was descended from beggars.

Still the wanderlust was on him and he vowed to

go even if he should die of hunger on the roadside. His mother loved him so much that she wanted to help him and so she went from one house to another explaining her plight. All in all she collected sixpence, gave it to him and wished him God speed.

He had gone a few miles when he met a man who asked him for alms and he gave him a little of his money and went on. Then he met another man who begged for something and he gave him some more and went on. By the time he met the third beggar he was reluctant to part with any of his money.

'I have hardly anything left,' he said.

The beggar said that they would go together to the inn and would buy something and eat it together as friends. In the inn they ordered bread and milk and while they were eating he told the beggar man his story; how he had always dreamed of adventure and how he was setting out for the lord's house in the hope of wooing the daughter. Now they ate and drank ravenously because they were so hungry but Marteen noticed something very extraordinary and it was this: the loaf didn't get any smaller and neither did the measure of milk, so much so that when the landlady came out she remarked that they had eaten nothing and she refused to take any money from them. Marteen insisted that she take a little and she blessed him for his good heart and sent him with a drop of holy water on his way.

Before they parted the beggar said to Marteen that he had been good to him three times on his journey since in fact he was the same beggar in different disguises, and as a reward he pulled from deep inside his pocket a gold ring and said, 'Wherever you place that ring and make a wish, gold will come.'

As he was speaking the beggar walked into the solid earth with the same ease as if passing through a bead curtain. Marteen put the ring into his pocket and straightaway it bulged out with gold, he then put it into his other pocket and the same thing happened and there he was walking along with two finikins of gold, chuckling at his good luck. When he got to the town he brought himself a serge suit, a white shirt with a stiff collar, a peaked cap and a hunter watch. He also bought a doctor's bag in which to carry his gold. He then set out for the lord's palace which was on the outskirts of the town. It was a palace made of pink stone with waterfalls on either side and peacocks in the front garden unfurling their tails and letting out their mysterious cries. He walked like a toff up the front steps and because of being dressed so smartly and talking so fluently he was admitted and made such an impression on the lord that it was assumed that he was a king's son.

The young daughter linked him as they went in to dinner and joked with him about being so educated. He drank the wine in great gulps and felt himself to be falling in love with the young girl, but due to intoxication he fell asleep and had to be carried to bed by the servants. On the way the ring slipped off his finger and the lord's daughter found it. She was going to keep it safely for him and was just admiring it when her stepsister pounced on her.

'Give me that,' said the stepsister, 'I'll keep it for him.'

'No you won't,' said the daughter, and they had a tussle over it and the stepsister got it and ran to her room and locked her door. To her great delight she found that the casket where she placed it filled up with gold and that when she put it into the washbasin the same thing happened, and finally she stuffed it into her wardrobe which began to bulge with gold bars.

When the daughter asked the stepsister in the morning to give the ring back she said she had thrown it in the lake because it was an unlucky ring.

Marteen wakened and was horrified to find his ring missing. He went to the kitchen and asked the servants, he then asked the lord's daughter but all in vain. What he couldn't understand was why the lord's daughter blushed and ran away from him. A sad man he was having lost both his ring and her affection. He decided to go home.

On his way he chanced upon three talking cats. Soon they were joined by a fourth cat who had just come from the lord's castle and was all agog relaying the story of what had happened to her in the castle and of what could be done to avert a tragedy, which she had caused by accident. As she was invisibly leaping about the room the lord's knife struck her tail and three drops of blood fell into his venison which he ate without realising it. As a result the lord had three kittens inside of him and was dying of an agony that could not be cured until he drank three draughts of water from the boundary well of Coolawn.

Now this well was near to Marteen's home so he

hurried on and got his mother to fill three bottles from the well and he set out again for the lord's house. There were doctors and nurses around the lord's bedside but none of them knew what to do and there was he, roaring like billyo.

'I'll cure him,' said Marteen and asked to be left alone with the patient.

He then made him drink from the three bottles and out jumped the kittens and bolted up the chimney. Within minutes the lord was up and well and asking for oysters. Marteen endeavoured again to get his ring back but the daughter explained that she did not have it. In fact it was spawning gold in the stepsister's room but no one knew. He said goodbye to them and set off hoping he might remeet the beggar man, who had given it to him in the first place.

He was walking through a dense wood when he heard some fighting and he came upon three boys, boxing each other under an oak tree. He asked them what the fight was about and they told him that their father had buried a ring somewhere under that tree, a ring by which you could be in any place in two minutes. Along with the ring there was a goblet that was always full and a harp that could play any tune it was told to.

'I want us to divide these treasures,' said the youngest boy.

'So do I,' said the middle boy.

'But I have a right to the lot,' said the eldest and so they started sparring again.

Marteen told them to go home and that if they came back on the morrow he would sort it out for them and find a solution to their quarrel. So the boys promised to be peaceable until they met next day. When they were gone, he went to an old farmyard nearby, found a shovel and came back and dug and dug until he found the ring, the goblet and the harp, buried under clay and flint.

The ring had the powers to transport him anywhere in two minutes, so he made the wish and immediately was knocking on the lord's door and being admitted. He was invited to join the lords and ladies as they went in to dinner.

He called on his harp to amuse the assembled company with various tunes, he drank from his goblet which was always full and unfortunately his head became heavy and once again he fell asleep and had to be put to bed. Now while he was asleep the step-sister took the ring off his finger, took the harp and the goblet and hid them in her chambers. Marteen was horrified when he wakened up. Again he asked the servants and he asked the daughter but they all pleaded ignorance and so he set out for home.

He walked and he walked until he came to a wild orchard where there were apples growing. On some trees the apples were bright red and on others they were golden russet. Being hungry and thirsty he plucked a red apple and ate it. As he was eating he felt a great disturbance in his head – 'Crunch, Crunch' – and then he felt some protuberances and when he put his hand up he found that he had sprouted two great horns. He ran down to the lake to take a look at himself and was delirious with fright. Some little voice inside him told him to eat one of the golden russet

apples and as he did there was another almighty 'Crunch, Crunch' and the horns snapped and fell at his feet.

So he filled two bags, one with red apples, the other with golden apples, and he set out for the lord's palace. When the guests saw the little bright red apples they asked for some and soon there was not a person in the palace that had not sprouted horns. Pandemonium followed. They ran about shrieking, convinced that they had been turned into devils. The lord asked Marteen in God's name to give them back their human

countenances and promised any reward necessary.

The daughter began to cry. She looked quite pathetic with tears dropping on to her bright green horns. Some horns had grown so long that their owners began to butt the floor like wild animals. The lamentations filled the hall as they begged Marteen to relent.

'Not unless I have my rings, my goblet and my harp back,' said Marteen, adamantly.

'Who has them?' asked the lord, trying to be majestic but his silly horns made him quite absurd-looking.

'She has them,' said the daughter, pointing to her stepsister whose horns were a very nasty purple, magenta even.

'Villanous,' said the lord and he dispatched her to get them.

The two rings, the goblet and the harp were brought before Marteen and then the lord placed his daughter's hand in Marteen's and said, 'She is yours, make her obey you.'

Marteen opened the second bag and gave each of them a golden apple. At once the horns snapped off and fell to the floor where they were gathered into a big heap. The crowd began to chant and intone a song of praise as they formed a chain and danced around the pyre to the strains of the melodious harp. The daughter squeezed Marteen's hand and with her big blue limpid eyes conveyed her love to him. He chuckled to himself, knowing at last that all his wishes had come true – the daughter's heart beat with love and gratitude towards him and they had as much

49

gold as they would need for the whole of their lives. As for the stepsister, she was sent to the kitchen where she would have to do a year's hard work as penance for her wicked deed.

The lord called Marteen aside and asked him how he had come to be so powerful. Marteen explained about the beggar and the buried treasure; but he did not know *why* he had come by them, why he was chosen above all the other young lads in the country.

He could only put it down to good luck, and good luck is something you're born with.

## The Lad with the Goatskin

Long ago there was a poor woman and she worked
at scrubbing but she was so poor she had no
clothes to put on her son Eamonn, so what she did
was to stick him down in the ash hole near the fire,
and pile the ashes around him to keep him warm. As
he began to grow she sunk the pit deeper and deeper
until he was in the ashes up to his shoulders. Well, at
any rate the work got a bit better because a big family
came to live in the neighbourhood and one day when
they were throwing things out didn't the widow
woman get a nice dappled goat skin. She brought it
home, she picked her son up out of the ashes and
fastened it around his waist. He was much taller than
she thought and as he was about eighteen years she
decided to put him to work. She handed him a bit of
rope and told him to go into the woods and bring
back some kindling and some firewood.

When Eamonn had gathered as much wood as he
wanted up comes a big giant nine foot high and takes
a lick at him with a club. Eamonn jumped aside,

51

picked up a log himself and gave the giant such a blow that he was kissing a clod of earth against his will.

'If you have a prayer,' said Eamonn, 'now is the time to utter it before I make a brisce of you.'

'I'll tell you what,' said the giant, 'if you save my life, I'll give you my club and you'll win every battle you'll fight with it.'

Soon as the giant had gone Eamonn struck the pile of wood with the club and said, 'I had a great bother getting you. Carry me home.'

Even as he said it he was swept up and carried through the air with the wood as his rocking horse.

A couple of days later Eamonn was sent to pick more wood and this time he had a fight with a giant that had two heads on him. It was a more arduous fight but he had the magic club and in due course the giant was on the ground and with his two mouths was asking Eamonn to spare his life.

'What will you give me?' said Eamonn. The giant produced a magic fife and said that nobody could help dancing when they heard it so Eamonn danced home with the wood dancing along beside him.

The third time Eamonn went into the woods he met a giant with three heads and after beating him he received a jar of green ointment that wouldn't let you be burned or scalded or bitten or wounded. However, he learned from this giant that there were no more of them in the woods and that he would receive no more booty.

brisce – a blob

Some time after, a man passed their gate blowing a big bugle and he proclaimed that the King of Dublin's daughter was so melancholy that she hadn't laughed for seven years and that her father would grant her in marriage to whoever could make her laugh three times.

'That's something for me to try,' said Eamonn and he kissed his mother, picked up his club and his fife and his green ointment and set off along the high road to Dublin.

At last Eamonn came to one of the city gates and the guards refused to let him in. He stood there and one of the guards drew a bayonet and drove it into his side. Eamonn did nothing except take the fellow by the scruff of his neck and toss him into the canal. Some of the guards ran to rescue their comrade while others tackled Eamonn with their daggers. A tap from his club sent them tumbling to the ground and they were soon begging him to pass on, to go into the city and to leave them alone. Now Eamonn made his way to the palace yard and there he saw the King and the Queen and the Princess, up in a gallery looking down at some entertainments. There was wrestling and sword playing and dancing and mumming, all to please the Princess, but not a smile bore down on her serious face.

Everyone looked when they saw the strong young man with his long black hair and his strong arms and a goatskin that reached from his waist to his knees. One young man in the crowd did not like the way the Princess looked at Eamonn, the way she opened her eyes wide as if she was about to smile. The young

man whose name was Fiac came across to Eamonn and asked him his business.

'My business,' said Eamonn, 'is to make the beautiful Princess laugh three times.'

'Nonsense,' said Fiac and pointed to the clowns and jugglers and swordsmen who had not got a laugh out of her for seven years.

'I'll make her laugh,' said Eamonn and by now a crowd had gathered around him to taunt him about his boast.

'You're an impostor,' they said.

'I don't care a pinch of snuff for any of you,' Eamonn said and put out his hands to box them.

Now the King called across to enquire what the stranger wanted.

'He wants,' said Fiac, 'to make pulp of your best men.'

'Tackle him,' said the King, annoyed at the audacity of the interloper. A knight came forward with his sword, using a pot lid as a shield and he took a swipe at Eamonn. Eamonn just struck the knight with his club and away flew the sword and down went the knight, much to the surprise of all. Another took his place and another and another but each time Eamonn sent swords and helmets and pot lids flying about and fellows were stretched on the floor crying that they were 'moidered'. The way they bawled like babies made the Princess laugh, as she had always seen them full of airs and graces.

'King of Dublin,' said Eamonn. 'I have a quarter of your daughter,'

The King looked stern but the daughter was

amused. The sunlight was falling on her so that her gold hair shone brightly and as she thumbed at one of her long plaits she asked her father a favour.

'Might the stranger have dinner with the royal family?'

It was during dinner that Eamonn heard tell of a wolf who marauded the palace and attacked cattle and people alike. Eamonn vowed that he would deal with the wolf. Hearing this the Princess became a little startled because secretly she was starting to fall in love with him. The thing is they had dressed him for dinner and he looked extremely smart in his velvet jacket with his long hair falling on to his shoulders.

The next day the wolf came into the palace yard and Eamonn took a step or two towards him as casually as if he was meeting a sheep. All the other people, including the King, the Queen and the Princess, were sheltering up in the gallery. The wolf snapped and slavered and gave a leap as if he was going to tear Eamonn to pieces. Everyone expected that it was with his club Eamonn would defend himself but not a bit of it. He took the fife from his pocket and began to play a jig. The minute the music started the wolf got on his hind legs and danced about. First he was dancing slowly but as Eamonn increased the pitch he began to dance wildly and had the most audacious steps. Now Fiac who did not know any of this came wandering through the front door and didn't the wolf petition him to a dance. Fiac had no choice. There they were, cheek to cheek and bosom to bosom doing a highland fling. One leg up and the other leg down, hold your partner and don't let go.

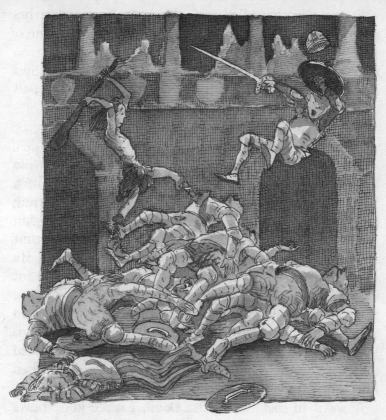

The Princess was in stitches and Eamonn took the
flute from his mouth to tell the King of Dublin that he
now owned half his daughter.

'Half or no half,' said the King, 'get rid of that wolf
because it's the hoight of trepidation we're all in.' So
Eamonn put the fife in his pocket and said to the beast
who was still careering around, 'Get off you curra-
bingo and hie to the Sugarloaf Mountains, and live like
a respectable baste.' He gave the wolf a blow of his
club and off he went, as meek as a lamb.

Everyone rejoiced except of course Fiac who was jealous.

'What next your lordship,' said Eamonn to the King. The King told him that his next task was to find a flail hanging on a beam in hell. It was the only flail that could keep the Danes away.

'What will you give me if I bring the flail to you?'

'I'll give you my daughter,' said the King.

The Princess did not want Eamonn to risk his life by going to hell but he told her not to worry as he'd be back in no time, as right as rain. It was a long journey through lonely country and he was glad when he came in sight of the wobbly bridge that stretched over miles and miles of black puddle. He saw the towering flames in the distance and as he got nearer he saw the guards with mangy dogs on leads. He pulled off his goatskin, rubbed himself from head to toe with the green ointment and proceeded on. When he knocked on the door a score of black-faced imps poked their heads through the bars and asked him what he wanted.

'I want to speak with the Devil, I have good news for him,' he said. The gates were pulled back and he was allowed in. He saw the Devil in his black robe, his face covered in a black caul and his eyes like two red cinders. The poor inmates were bound to pillars with flames leaping up to their cheeks and haloes of fire all around their hair.

'What do you want?' asked the Devil.

'I want the loan of that flail that I see hanging on the collar beam. It's for the King of Dublin to thrash the Danes.'

'What will I get in return?' asked the Devil.

'You'll get a lot of dead Danes,' said Eamonn.

The Devil ordered his men to hand over the flail knowing that it was boiling hot. He grinned at the prospect of Eamonn burning his hands off. Of course, because of the ointment the burning flail did him no harm.

'Much obliged,' said Eamonn and he proceeded to go out. Now the imps had locked the door and another batch of imps were coming at him with pots of boiling oil. Eamonn raised his club and tore into them. Such shouting and clobbering and hussaing you never heard. So much so that the Devil ordered to let him go because he was bringing nothing but havoc.

Off marched Eamonn with shouts and curses from all sides, and when he arrived back at the palace a crowd ran forward to greet him. He put the flail down on the stone stairs warning everybody not to touch it. The King walked towards it in utter amazement. The Queen and the Princess waved from the balcony. Everyone cheered except Fiac, the mean redhead, who stole over to catch hold of the flail in order to put an end to his rival. Well, didn't it cling to him so that he jumped in the air like a yo-yo and then fell to the ground saying that his fingers were roasting and begging Eamonn to take it off him.

'Throw it off,' said Eamonn.

'It's sthuck to me,' said Fiac.

'Oh, the devil must like you!' said Eamonn.

'No he doesn't,' said Fiac in a whimper.

'Why did you catch it?' said Eamonn.

'Curiosity,' said Fiac.

'You're lying,' said Eamonn.

'I'm not,' said Fiac.

'Then why does the Devil like you?' said Eamonn.

'I don't know,' said Fiac.

'You're a mean, lying, crooked, jealous, spineless, scut of a fellow,' said Eamonn lifting off the flail. Fiac looked at his two fingers that had been skinned.

'I want the skin of my fingers back,' said he.

'Go to hell for them,' said Eamonn, turning away, and everyone laughed but the Princess laughed louder than anyone. Eamonn did not have to ask the King again, because the Princess herself made her decision by walking towards him, placing her hands in his, and telling the assembled company that she had never met anyone so brave and so funny.

'I have never larned the rules of etiket,' said Eamonn, going down on one knee, 'so give me a thrifle of directions.' The Princess laughed again and the company could see that now she was most certainly his. They were betrothed there and then, and not only that but when the Danes learned that the King had got the flail out of hell they fled the country and took to their ships. Before he married, Eamonn insisted on learning the principles of politeness, fluxions, gunnery, decimal fractions, chess, science and *haute couture*.

## The Blue Bottle

There lived a poor man with his wife and several children and they had to exist on the scrapings from their few acres of rocky land. One summer there was torrential rain – the oats they had sown got destroyed, the chickens died of the pip, the pig got pneumonia and the poor man didn't have the money to pay his rent.

'Oh, Mary, what shall we do?' said he to his wife.

'Wisha, then, mavoureen, what can we do but sell the cow?'

'What will we do when she's gone?' said he.

'We'll have to trust in God,' said she.

So the next day he set out for the fair of Cork. His wife shook holy water on himself and the beast and it was a long and a lonesome walk he had, talking to the cow to keep himself company.

61

He found himself in the middle of a lonely moor and came to a spot where there was a clump of hazel trees. He thought he heard a whistle, something similar to the curlew's cry, and then the cow shied and tried to break away. Before his eyes there sauntered forth a little man about three feet high in a frieze coat that came to the ground. He had a wrinkled face, skin the colour of cauliflower, no nose and little scalding eyes.

'Where are you going with the cow?' said he in a piping voice.

'I'm having to sell her,' said the farmer, flabbergasted at the sight of the stranger.

'That means you have no money,' said the little man. 'I could give you this bottle,' said he, producing a dark blue bottle from under his coat. It was a humble-looking thing such as you would find tossed in any ditch.

'It's worth thousands of pounds,' said the little man.

'Do you think I'm a fool?' said the farmer.

'You won't be sorry if you take it,' said the little man.

'It's money I need,' said the farmer.

'This bottle is better than any money, Mick Boland,'

Mick started and asked the little man how he knew his name.

'I know you and I have a regard for you,' said he and then pointing to the cow he said it wouldn't surprise him if she didn't die of hunger and exhaustion before they got to the fair at all.

'You're trying to worry me,' said Mick.

'I'm trying to bring you good luck,' said the little man.

'Faith, I need luck,' said Mick as he thought on how destitute they were.

'Then give me the cow and take the bottle and when you go home do as I say.'

Mick was in a quandary because he was half-believing the little man.

'Take it and be rich, refuse it and be a pauper.'

Mick stared at him, trying to decide; then all of a sudden he seized the bottle and said, 'If you're lying to me the curse of the poor will be on you.'

'I have spoken the truth and now you must do what I tell you,'

'What's that?' said Mick.

'When you go home, never mind if your wife is angry, get her to sweep the floor, set a cloth on the table and put the bottle on the ground saying these words, "Bottle do your duty." '

'Is that all?' said Mick.

'That's it,' said the stranger, 'off with you now, and rejoice – you're a rich man.

'God grant it,' said Mick as he saw his cow being driven away. He began to retrace his steps but when he looked back neither the cow nor the man was to be seen.

He went on home muttering prayers and holding on to his bottle. At one point he slipped and thought it had broken, so after that he put it inside his shirt, next to his skin. He kept thinking about the trouble he'd be in with his wife and at the same time speculating on the powers of the bottle.

'Oh Mick, you're back,' said his wife, surprised that he'd been there and back so soon. She asked who bought the cow and how much money he got.

'I don't know who bought her,' said Mick, wondering how he'd tell his tale and dreading her temper.

'But where's the money?' said she.

'Be quiet now,' said he and took out the bottle and laid it on the table. 'That's what I got for the cow.'

'Oh you fool and you bostoon,' said she and asked in the name of God how they would pay their rent and what they would eat for their supper.

'Be patient,' said he and he told her about the strange little man and the promises he'd made.

'Blood and blunderbusses,' said she and she seized the bottle and would have broken it but that he grasped it from her and held it tight. Then he told her the story from start to finish. Whether it was the way he told it or whether it was that the poor desperate woman would try any remedy, she got up quietly, she began to sweep the floor, she tidied around, she pulled out the table, she spread the cloth on it and then waited anxiously. Mick put the bottle on the ground, pointed his finger at it and said 'Bottle do your duty.'

'Look, look,' said one of their little children, as two tiny little sprites rose up out of the bottle and in an instant covered the table with gold plates and dishes, then filled the plates with the most delicious roast and victuals and put jugs of ale down. Having done that they slid back down into the bottle again and Mick and his family sat down at the table to eat.

''Tis a long road that has no turning,' said Mick, prouder than he had ever been.

'I wonder if they'll take these gold dishes away,' said Mary and they waited but no one came.

A few days later Mick sold the gold plates and with the money bought a horse and cart, and warm clothes for his children. No matter what they wanted, Mick had only to say 'Bottle do your duty' and it was granted. The word got around that they were beginning to show signs of great prosperity so the landlord drove over one day and asked Mick where he suddenly got his money.

'It's not from a few barren acres of land,' said the landlord.

Mick couldn't help boasting about the bottle and of course as he did the landlord coveted it. He offered Mick a great deal of money but Mick did not need money. Then he offered him a big farm with stables and cattle on the land and Mick was not able to refuse it. He would be a gentleman at last. He handed over the bottle and very soon was installed in his new farm. He lived lavishly, invented a coat of arms for himself, sent to France for wine, to Russia for caviar and to Italy for marble mantelpieces and furniture. As time went on his money ran out, his friends began to desert him and soon he was a pauper.

Mick and his wife decided that he should do as before, that he should set out for the fair with his only cow, that he should take the exact same route and that most likely he'd meet his little man.

It was very misty the morning he set out. He and the cow crossed the valley and then took the main road until they reached the track that led to the moor. He came to the hazel clump and sure enough the cow shied and he heard the voice of the little man.

'I told you you'd be rich,' said the little man.

'I'm not rich now,' said Mick. 'I want another bottle and I'll give you this cow,'

'Here you are,' said the little man. 'And you know what to do with it.'

Mick ran as fast he could, eager to set his bottle down at home and bedeck himself with fine things and loot. Seeing him come in such excitement, his wife ran out to meet him.

Once at home his wife did as before. She swept the floor, put the cloth on the table and waited for Mick to give the order.

'Bottle do your duty.'

Well as soon as he said it, two strong hoboes with big cudgels came out of the bottle and struck Mick a blow, then his wife, then all the bairns, till they lay in a heap on the floor yelling and roaring. Soon as he came to his senses, Mick got up and was relieved to find that the hoboes had gone back into the bottle and all was quiet except for his children mewling. He picked up the bottle, put it inside his vest and set off for the landlord's house. A servant met him at the door and wasn't at all inclined to let him in.

'Tell your master I have another bottle,' said Mick.

'Capital . . . capital,' said the servant and he led him into the great hall.

The landlord was having his breakfast and when Mick told him the news the landlord asked if it was as good as the first.

'It's better,' said Mick.

He could see his own bottle up on the mantelshelf and was thinking to himself that it would shortly be in his possession.

'Show us,' said the landlord.

Mick set the second bottle on the table and gave the instructions. Out stepped the two villains and in no time the landlord and his family were sprawled on the floor with crockery and fried eggs and porridge heaped over them.

'Stop these devils, Mick Boland, or I'll have you hanged,' said the landlord from under the table.

'I won't stop them till I get my own bottle back,' said Mick.

'Take it and clear out,' said the landlord.

Mick jumped on a chair, picked up his own bottle, put it inside his shirt and ordered the two villains to create a bit more rumpus in order to give him a chance to escape.

As he was crossing the moor he met with the little man.

'Let me see the bottle to make sure it came to no harm.'

As soon as Mick handed it over he saw the little man grinning and cuddling it to his chest and he knew that he was not going to get it back.

'Give me one last chance,' he begged.

'You've had your chance.'

'I was a fool,' said Mick.

'Aye,' laughed the little man and without further ado he disappeared and in his place there stood a bit of a broken tree with a crow cawing on it and staring at Mick with blood-red eyes. Mick called and called but only the crow answered. They named the spot 'Bealnabuideal' (the mouth of the bottle) and there are people that still believe that on some lonesome journey, some poor farmer will meet the little man who will give him the bottle in exchange for a cow.

## Hookedy Crookedy

Once upon a time there was a king and a queen and they had one son named Jack and as he got older he said to his parents that he would go out into the world and seek his fortune. They didn't want him to go, of course, but they couldn't stop him so they gave him his blessing and off he started. After a while he came to a big wood and he met a grey-haired man and the man said, 'Where are you going?' and he said, 'I'm going to seek my fortune.'

'Well,' said the man, 'I have a piece of advice for you. There's a giant who lives at the opposite end of this wood. He's called the Giant of the Hills and he wants a nice, fine, strong, clever, young fellow.'

'All right,' said Jack, 'I'll go to him.'

So he went through the wood until he got to the other side and he saw the giant's castle and he knocked on the door and a big giant came out.

'Welcome,' said the giant to the king's son, 'what have you come for? What do you want?' and Jack told

70

him that he had come to look for honest service and he said that he had been told that the giant wanted a willing and clever boy.

'Well,' said the giant, 'I am the Giant of the Hills and I do want such a fine fellow because I have to go from here every day to do battle with one giant or another and when I'm away I want somebody to look after my house and my grounds and my farm buildings and if you will be good and faithful and do everything I tell you I'll give you a bit of gold at the end of your service.'

Jack promised that he would do all that and the giant gave him a supper of meat and broth and a drop of wine. Then he slept soundly that night and he was up in the morning before the lark.

'Now Jack,' said the giant to him. 'I've to be at the other end of the country today to fight the Giant of the Winds so it's time you were up and attending to business. You have to put this house in order and you're to look after everything until I come back. Now you can go anywhere you like in the house or in the outhouses except for the stable. The stable door is closed and on peril of your life don't open that door and don't go into the stable.'

Jack said he would certainly do as he was told and the giant went off on his fight. Now as soon as he was gone Jack was fixing and arranging things in the house. He did the dishes, he swept the floor, he brought wood and turf in for the fire and then he went out into the yard and looked in at all the buildings except of course the stable. But as the day wore on his curiosity got the better of him and he said

71

to himself, 'I wonder what can be in there, what is the reason that he wants me, on peril of my life, not to go in. I'd love to have a peep at it.'

So he tried the door, and eventually he found a way of opening it, by twisting and turning the lock with a little sprig of wire.

When the door flew open he found, to his surprise, that there was no gold or treasure in there. What he sees in fact is a mare and a bear and they're standing by the manger but neither of them is eating. They're looking extremely sad and morose and when he looks into the manger he sees there's hay in front of the bear and there's meat in front of the mare.

'Oh,' says he, 'it's no wonder the poor creatures aren't eating.' He changed their food, putting the hay in front of the mare and the meat in front of the bear, and immediately the two of them started to eat like gluttons and Jack came out of the stable and closed the door. Now as he was locking it his finger stuck in the pivot and he pulled and he jerked and he struggled to get it away but he couldn't.

'Oh,' he thought to himself, 'if the giant comes back and finds me stuck here that'll be bad news.' So what does he do, the brave Jack, but he whips out his penknife, cuts off his finger and leaves it there.

Now when the giant came home that night from battle he washed himself in a big tub and said to Jack, 'What sort of a day have you had and how did you get on?'

'Well, I had a fine day,' said Jack, 'got on very well indeed,'

'Jack,' says the giant, 'show me your two hands.'

And when Jack held out his two hands the giant saw that the index finger of one was gone. He got black in the face with a rage and he said, 'Didn't I tell you on peril of your life not to go into that stable?'

So Jack was very contrite and said he hadn't meant to, or anything, but that he just really thought he'd open the door and have a peep in. The giant looked even crosser and said, 'Anyone that has ever opened that door up to now has been killed and I would kill you this very instant except that your father's father, a king, once did me a great service and I am a man who never forgets a good thing so this time I pardon you your life, but if you do it again you will not live.'

Now Jack promised he'd never do it again and so they had their supper and went to bed and early next morning the giant got up and roused Jack and announced, 'I must be off to another brawl today; you know your duty. Look after the house and the place, put everything in order, go anywhere you like, but don't go into the stable.'

'Certainly, Sir,' said Jack. The giant went into the stable before he left, then after he had gone, Jack set to work cleaning and sweeping up. At noon he went into the yard and when he came to the stable he stood and he listened at the door. He thought, 'I wonder what the giant did when he went in there.'

Again curiosity got the better of him and he decided to unlock the door. He saw the mare and the bear as before, standing by the manger in a sullen and morose state. The meat was in front of the mare and the hay was in front of the bear, so he changed the food, putting the hay before the mare and the meat before

the bear and very soon they were eating heartily. He
went out and he closed the door and as he did, his
finger stuck in the pivot again, and pull and tug as he
did, he could not get it out.

'Oh,' he cries, 'I'm a dead man tonight, surely.'

So all he could do was whip out his penknife and
cut off the next finger and leave it there.

The giant came home at nightfall and he bellowed
out, 'Well, how did you get on today?'

'Oh, fine, fine,' said Jack as he hid his hands behind
his back.

'Show me your hands, Jack,' said the giant.

When Jack showed his hands with the two fingers
missing the giant erupted.

'I forgave you yesterday for going into that stable
and you promised not to go again, and now I find you
out once more.' So he raged and he shouted and
eventually he calmed down a bit and he relented.
'Because your father's father did me such a good
turn, I'll spare your life this time but if you should live
for a hundred years don't ever go into that stable
again.'

In the morning the giant went into the stable
before leaving. When he was gone Jack went around
the house and around the yard putting everything in
order and still he couldn't stop himself, it was as if
some spell was on him because as he got to the stable
door he thought 'I wonder how the poor creatures are
getting on and why the giant goes in there every morning.'

He decided to risk it, and it was the same as the two
previous days. The food was changed around, the

meat before the mare and the hay before the bear.

'Poor creatures,' said Jack, and he went and changed it, placing the food where it should be, the hay before the mare and the meat before the bear when up speaks the mare.

'Oh, poor Jack,' says she, 'I am sorry for you because this night you will surely be killed. I'm sorry for us too for we'll be killed as well as you.'

'Oh,' says Jack, 'is there nothing we can do?'

'There is only one thing,' says the mare.

'What is it?' says Jack.

'It is this,' says the mare. 'Put my saddle and bridle on and let us start off and go far away from this place and be gone when the giant comes back,'

So Jack put the saddle and the bridle on the mare and he was riding out of the stable when the bear grunted.

'Oh, the two of you are going to leave me alone in this dungeon.'

'No,' says the mare, 'we will not do that.'

'Jack,' says she, 'take the chains off the bear and tie them to the reins.'

So Jack released the bear, hitched her up and the three of them set off. Jack galloped as fast as he could and after a while he thought he heard someone calling his name.

'Look behind you and see what you can see,' says the mare.

'Oh,' says he, 'I see the giant coming after us pell-mell and he's overtaking us and we'll be murdered.'

Says the mare, 'Look in my left ear and see what you can see.'

He looked inside her left ear and he saw a little shiny chestnut.

'Snatch it out and throw it over your left shoulder,' says the mare.

So Jack snatches it out, throws it over his left shoulder and a huge chestnut wood about eight or nine miles in length and breadth rears up behind them. So they rode on that day and that night. The next day as they were galloping away the mare says, 'Jack, look behind you and see what you can see.'

Jack looked behind him and he let out another shriek because it was the giant tearing after them like a hurricane.

'Do you see anything strange about him, Jack?' says the mare.

'Yes,' says Jack, 'there's a whole lot of furze bushes on top of his head and there's a whole lot of fowl and game stuck about his feet and his legs so that he has enough firewood and he has enough flesh for years to come. We're done for.'

'Not yet,' says the mare. 'Look into my right ear and see what you can see.'

So he looks into the mare's right ear and sees a drop of silver-coloured water.

'Throw it over your left shoulder, Jack,' says the mare, 'and see what will happen!'

Over his left shoulder Jack throws it and as he does there springs up a lake a hundred miles wide and a hundred miles deep.

'Now,' says the mare, 'he can't reach us until he drinks his way through that lake and if he drinks that much he'll burst, so we'll be shut of him altogether.'

So on they went until they reached Ulster at the very opposite end of the country and when they came to an oak wood the mare told him to dismount.

'Now,' said the mare to the bear, 'this wood is to be our hiding place.'

'But what about me?' said Jack. 'I can't hide in a wood, I can't eat hay or berries.'

'Oh you, Jack,' said the mare, 'you must push on. You have to get employment.' She said, 'There's a king in this province and I think you'd be likely to get employment there, but first I have to do something terrible to you.'

'Oh,' said Jack, 'what?'

'I have to change you into a little crooked fellow because the King has three beautiful daughters and he won't take into service any man as handsome as you in case one of his daughters would fall in love with you.'

Then, before Jack could disagree, the mare came very close to him, she put her nostrils on his breast, she blew out and all of a sudden he was turned into this little wizened ugly hookedy crookedy fellow.

'Jack,' says the mare, 'before you go, look in my left ear and take what you find there.'

Now out of the left ear of the mare he took a little cap and she explained to him, 'This is a wishing cap and every time you put it on and wish to have anything done it will be done, and whenever you're in any trouble come back here and I'll do what I can for you.'

So Jack said goodbye to the mare and the bear and he set off and he crossed through the woods and the next day he came to the castle and he walked up to it and went to the back door and said he wanted employment. He was told by a woman there that the King of Ulster would not employ any man in the house, but he said that he was so ugly being a hookedy crookedy little fellow that the King might employ him. So the woman went off to ask the King and Jack put on his wishing cap and wished that all the cutlery would be cleaned and polished, all the knives and all the forks and the soup-spoons and the tea-spoons and the egg-spoons, and it was done in a flash.

When the King came and saw that Jack had cleaned all that cutlery so quickly he agreed to keep him in service but, in order to be on the safe side, the King brought down his three daughters to see the impression that Jack made on them. Well, when they came into the kitchen in their finery and they saw this little dwarf standing near the fireplace, tiny and gnarled looking, with little hands and a little black snout of a nose, they bolted.

So the King was very pleased by that and said to Jack that yes, he had employment, and he sent him out into the garden to work. Now at this time another king had declared war on the King of Ulster and this was the King of the Goths. He had a mighty army and he threatened to slay the King of Ulster and rule over the province. The King of Ulster was livid and he called in his Grand Adviser and he asked his Grand Adviser what was the best thing to do. The Grand Adviser said he should give his three daughters in marriage to sons of different kings because in that way he would have an army, he would have the support of the kings his daughters married.

So the King of Ulster sent messengers to all parts of the world to say he had beautiful daughters and they were eligible for marriage and in a very short time the Prince of Spain came and married the eldest daughter, the Prince of France came and he married the second daughter, and a whole lot of princes came wooing the youngest who was beautiful and whose name was White Rose. She wouldn't take any one of the suitors. With this the King ordered her out of his sight and said she was never to come into his company again.

So White Rose was banished from the castle and she spent all her time now wandering in the garden and slept in a little hut there. The only person she had

for a friend was Hookedy Crookedy because he was looking after the vegetables and flowers. So every day she'd come around and she'd chat to him and as time went on Hookedy Crookedy noticed that she was coming more often and she'd bring him little presents and she'd blush when she saw him. To his utter astonishment he realised that she was falling in love with him. In fact he was in love with her too.

The Grand Adviser told the King that he should send the two princes, his sons-in-law the Prince of Spain and the Prince of France, to the Well at the World's End, to get bottles of Ioccaha water. They were to take these bottles to battle with them because the liquid would cure the wounded and even dead men. So the King ordered his sons-in-law to go to the Well at the World's End and bring back the two bottles.

Now White Rose had some friends still in the palace and she was told this story about the two princes going to the Well at the World's End and she repeated it to Hookedy Crookedy. Now Hookedy Crookedy thought, 'There's a bit of magic afoot here,' and he decided to go back into the woods and search out the mare and the bear to get advice.

So, off he went and the mare and the bear were thrilled to see him. He told them the things that had happened and how the King's two sons-in-law were going to the Well at the World's End to get the Ioccaha water.

'Well, Jack,' said the mare, 'I want you to go with the two princes. When you go, take an old hunter in

Ioccaha – healing water

the King's stable, an old bony, scrawny animal that's past work; put a straw saddle on him and dress yourself up in the most terrible clothes, rags really. Then you'll meet up with the two men on the road and tell them that you're going with them. Oh, they'll be very ashamed of you and they'll be ashamed of your horse and they'll do everything to get rid of you. One of them will propose going to have a drink and while you're having the drink will suggest that the three of you separate, that each one of you takes a different road to the Well. Whoever is back first with a bottle of water is the hero.'

Then the mare warned him that they were dishonest princes and that they would not go to the Well at the World's End but that they would fill their bottles from the first well they came to and pretend to the King that it was Ioccaha.

'Villains,' said Hookedy Crookedy.

'Never mind,' said the mare and then she told him that he would be the hero.

'After the three of you have parted and you have gone around the first bend you are to put on that wishing cap and you are to wish the two bottles of the Ioccaha water from the Well at the World's End and at once two bottles will appear.'

Jack thanked the mare and went back to the palace. The next day when the King's two sons-in-law set out on their quest they met up with Jack who was sitting on a very skinny old nag and, as the mare had predicted, they made fun of him. However when they came to the crossroads they proposed having a drink and, once inside, one of them suggested that they

each take a different road and that whoever got to the
Well first would be the hero. Naturally Jack agreed.
They each took a road and when Jack had gone
around the first bend, he put on his wishing cap. He
wished the two bottles of Ioccaha from the Well at the
World's End and no sooner had he wished it than two
dark green bottles appeared.

When he got to the palace the two princes were already there and they mocked him as he produced his two green round bottles. They said that he hadn't been to the Well at all, that he had cheated.

'I wonder,' said Jack, 'if that isn't your own story.' And he proposed a test. They would call in a servant, cut his head off and then cure him with water from one of the bottles. The two princes, knowing that they had cheated, refused to take part in the test. However Jack defied them.

A servant was called, whereupon Jack drew his sword, whipped the head off him and in minutes had it restored to him simply by pouring a few drops of water from one of the bottles.

The princes were flabbergasted. They asked Jack how much he wanted for his two bottles.

Said Jack, 'I will take the golden balls that are the surety of your marriage pledge and I will also ask you to permit me to write something on your backs.'

They didn't think that this was any great demand so they each handed over the golden ball that was their marriage token and they took off their shirts in order that Jack could write on their bare backs. Jack wrote: 'This man is unlawfully married.'

He gave them the bottles of Ioccaha and they brought them to the King and Jack went back to his garden. Now he didn't tell White Rose where he had been or what he was doing. He just said he was away on a message for her father. Meanwhile the King had got the bottles of Ioccaha and he gave orders that his army should prepare for battle.

The next day Jack decided to go into the woods

again to consult the mare. She said to him, 'Look in my left ear, Jack, and see what you will see.'

So he looked in the mare's left ear and took out of it the most wonderful soldier's uniform. The mare told him to put it on and get on her back. So he put the uniform on and as he did he was transformed into the most handsome, dashing soldier and off he and the mare went, away to the war. Everyone saw them coming and they admired Jack very much because he was so handsome and so well dressed and so brave and the word was mentioned to the King about some strange prince who had arrived with a mare and a bear.

The King and his men had gathered at a place called Fionntulagh which is the White Hill. Upon seeing the strange prince the King asked him which side he was on.

'I'm on your side,' said Jack, 'I'm on the side of the King of Ulster,'

The two sides set down their banners, the bugles sounded the warring cries as the soldiers picked up their clubs and their cudgels and went into the fray. Jack led the cavalry and he outshone all the others in his daring and his valour; men fell at his feet as readily as thistles. Towards the end of the day he met face to face with the King of the Goths and he made such an onslaught on him that the King and his men fled the field and rode into the hills for safety.

The King of Ulster was overjoyed and he invited Jack to come home with him to supper. Jack declined, saying that he was expected at home.

So the King said, 'The least I can do is give you a present.'

He gave Jack a tablecloth stating that every time he spread it out it would be laden with food and drink, of its own accord. Jack thanked him for his generosity and then rode into the woods, took off his uniform and became Hookedy Crookedy again.

He was in the garden digging the next day when White Rose told him how she had heard from the servants about this brave and mysterious soldier.

'Oh,' said Jack, 'he must be a very grand fellow. It's a pity I wasn't there.'

'Oh, poor Hookedy Crookedy,' said she, 'what could you do if you were there?'

Jack went into the woods again next day and he conferred with the mare.

'Jack,' said the mare, 'look in the inside of my left ear and see what you will see.'

And he took out of her left ear another soldier's suit. This time it was done up with silver and on the advice of the mare he donned it and they set out to battle. Everyone was amazed by the sight of another dashing stranger. The King addressed him and said, 'I think it was a brother of yours that came to us when we were last in battle.'

'That's right,' said Jack, 'he sent me to take his place.'

They rode into battle and again Jack commanded the men of Ulster. He was able to fend off a dozen hairy Goths at a time, while also giving orders and rousing cries whenever his men seemed in danger of faltering.

By nightfall the day was theirs and the King invited Jack to his castle saying he would give a feast in his honour. Jack declined, saying he was expected at home. Again the King gave him a present. It was a chain-mail purse. The King said, 'No matter how much or how often you have to pay, it will never be empty.'

Jack took the purse, rode into the woods, took off his uniform and became Hookedy Crookedy again.

When White Rose came into the garden the next day she raved about the mysterious soldier and the courage he had instilled into the men.

'I'm sorry I wasn't there, but I had to be away on an errand for your father,' said Hookedy Crookedy.

'Oh, my poor Hookedy Crookedy,' said she, 'what could you do if you were there?'

Well, a few days after that they heard that the King of the Goths had rallied a fresh army and that he was coming to battle with them again, so Jack went off to the woods to consult with the mare.

'Look in my left ear, Jack, and see what you will see.'

From the mare's left ear he took out the most beautiful uniform of all. It was scarlet with gold braiding and a boss of medals on either side. He rode into battle prouder than he had ever been and the King asked him to lead his men.

Fearful indeed was the fray which followed – bugle calls, the yells of the warriors, the breaking of shields, the flashing and clashing of swords and over it all the dazzling figure of Jack inciting his men and crushing his enemies. He marked the King of the Goths and hurled a stone at him which sank into his brain and made him tumble from his horse letting out a hideous groan.

The Goths retreated in shame and chaos. The King spoke to Jack, thanked him and said he'd never be able to repay him enough. He invited him to the castle to give a feast in his honour but Jack said that he couldn't go. He promised to come another time, and also to send his brothers.

'Let the three of you come together,' said the King.

'Oh, only one of us can leave home each day. I will come tomorrow and my second brother the day after and my third brother the day after that.'

The King accepted this and then presented Jack with a magic gift. It was a little silver comb with very special properties. He explained that every time Jack combed his hair, bushels of gold and silver would usher out and, another thing, it had the power to transform the ugliest man into a Prince. Jack thanked the King and he rode away delighted. So the King, as on the two previous days after the battle, cured the dead and the wounded with the bottles of Ioccaha water and all the men were well again. Jack rode into the woods, left the mare and the bear, and became Hookedy Crookedy again.

When he reported for work next morning White Rose was babbling on about the third hero who even surpassed his brothers in valour and fearlessness.

'Oh,' said Jack, 'I wish I'd been there, but I was away on an errand for your father.'

'Oh,' she said, 'poor Hookedy Crookedy, twas better you weren't because what could you do?'

So the next day Jack went into the woods to the mare and the bear, donned his military suit and rode to the castle for the feast. When he got there all the gates were closed but he put the mare at the walls

and he leapt over them. Now the King was cross
with the gatekeepers for not recognising him but
Jack said a trifle like that didn't bother him or harm
his mare.

During dinner the King asked him what he thought
of his daughters, and their husbands, and Jack said
they were very pleasant girls but wondered if there
were any other daughters in the family. The King said
that he had another daughter but that she would not
consent to marry any of the suitors he had chosen
and he banished her.

Jack insisted on seeing her. The King said he never
allowed her to enter the palace but since Jack kept
pleading the King yielded and so White Rose was sent
for. Now Jack was full of charm and looking so
splendid that she didn't recognise him as the ugly
little Hookedy Crookedy whom she conversed with
every day. He told her he had heard that she had the
bad luck to fall in love with a little crooked skalpeen
of a fellow in her father's garden. She seethed at that
and warned him to mind his own business.

'It is my business,' he said, and then declared his
intentions which were to ask for her hand in marriage.

She refused, saying that she was already betrothed.
'Also, I won't sit here and hear the man that I love
being ridiculed,' she shouted and rose to go.

'Brava,' said Jack, 'I admire your spirit, so let me
make you a little present before you go.' And he
handed her the tablecloth and he said, 'If you marry
your Hookedy Crookedy, as long as you have this
tablecloth neither of you will want for food.'

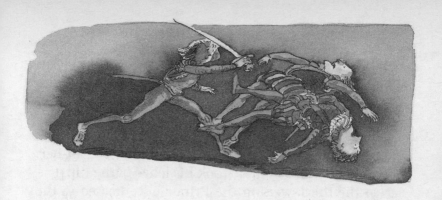

Her two jealous sisters tried to grab the tablecloth but Jack guarded it and pushed them away.

Now, the next evening for the dinner, Jack came in the dress in which he had gone into the second battle and he cleared the walls and came before the King and after dinner the King asked him what he thought of his daughters and their husbands. So Jack said they were very pleasant and asked if there were any other daughters in the family and the King said, 'I have one but I don't count her as my daughter any more because she's fallen in love with an ugly crooked little whelp of a fellow and I banished her from my sight.'

Jack claimed to be very curious about such an independent girl and added that he'd like to see her. The King eventually relented and she was led into the dining room, dressed in tatters. Jack did all he could to win her affections. He told her of his exploits in battle, of the treasures he had accrued, reminding her that if she married him she could live in luxury, a thing she wouldn't be able to do with Hookedy Crook-edy.

She reminded him that love was something that could neither be bought nor bartered for. Once more, impressed by her spirit he said it would be an honour to give her a present.

Her sisters went green when they saw him hand over the beautiful purse, a purse that would constantly replenish itself. Then he escorted her through the door so that her sisters could not snatch it from her. At midnight, as usual, he took his leave of the King.

On the third evening the Prince was dressed in the uniform which he had worn on the third day of the battle. After eating and drinking the King asked his opinion of his daughters and their husbands and Jack as usual pleaded that the wayward daughter be brought in. This time he did everything he could to win her heart. He recited an ode to her beauty, he produced a diamond ring and promised her that if she married him he would even give her a potion which would make her forget Hookedy Crookedy. She lost her temper. She said she had no intention of yielding to bribery and moreover that she did not want to forget Hookedy Crookedy because in her eyes he was the most handsome and noble man that ever lived. He was her destiny.

Undaunted, Jack said again that he'd like to make her a little present, so he gave her the comb, explaining, 'It will comb out of your hair a bushel of gold and a bushel of silver and besides it will make handsome the ugliest man that ever was.'

Now when the sisters heard this they shrieked and ordered their husbands to grab it but with some swift thrusts of his sword Jack knocked the husbands down senseless. The King was furious. 'How dare you dishonour the finest and bravest men in the world!'

'Fine and brave,' sneered Jack. 'They are worthless creatures. They are not even your lawful sons-in-law.'

'Impostor,' said the King.

'Strip their backs,' called Jack, 'and see for yourself.'

Their backs were stripped and their tunics pulled from them and there the King saw written, 'These Men Are Unlawfully Married.'

'What does this mean?' asked the King. 'They are married to my two daughters. They have golden tokens, golden balls to prove their marriage.'

Jack drew out of his pocket the golden balls and handed them to the King. The King was flabbergasted and Jack made him sit down until he heard the whole story. He admitted that he was in fact Hookedy Crookedy and though the King was a little disgruntled at having been deceived he soon forgave Jack because of his brave deeds. Although he did not like to be deceived it was something Hookedy Crookedy had to do and he welcomed him as a future son-in-law. Jack then took leave of the King and went into the woods to see the mare and the bear and to change his attire. Before long he returned to the garden as Hookedy Crookedy and when White Rose saw him she seemed very excited and asked if she could comb his hair.

He sat down on a garden seat and as she combed his hair out came streamers of silver and gold, and not only that, but his face began to change and his body became tall and strong. Hookedy Crookedy was no more. Instead she beheld the beautiful Prince who had tried three days in succession to woo her. At first she was frightened but Jack reassured her and explained the whole story, insofar as he himself understood it.

The King was overjoyed and arranged for a traditionally sumptuous wedding. Being summertime, it was held out of doors. Young men carried torches of dried bog-wood, and young maidens carried lighted rush candles, while behind followed a troop of boys with flutes and pipes and fiddles. The bridal pair walked hand in hand, a large canopy of white gauze held above their heads to celebrate the mystery of love. A youth shook meal from a sieve to wish them prosperity and fertility. Suddenly there appeared out of the bonfire a beautiful woman in a green silk dress wearing a green cloak with a golden brooch. She tried to separate them.

'Would you watch your manners,' said Jack.

'My manners are better than your memory, Hookedy Crookedy,' said she as she called him to one side.

Everyone shuddered because they knew that she was not a mortal woman and that she would try to lure him to the underworld. The Princess was the most terrified because she feared that her happiness was about to be destroyed. She need not have feared, because Jack was so resolute that the Faery Woman realised she could not charm him and so she withdrew, but not before telling him that she was the mare who had been his friend and who had hoped to marry him.

'Is this my reward?' she asked.

'You should not have helped me unless you wanted to,' Jack said.

At that she turned, raised a wand and was swept up into the sky in a silver curricle.

The procession then moved on to the ancient altar and having gone round it three times the canopy was lifted from the bridal pair and they were married before all the people. A wild chorus rose from the crowd, the musicians buckled on their pipes and the music and singing resounded throughout the whole countryside.

## Lord Mount Dhraggin

Once upon a time there was a little weaver, a very honest and industrious man with a wife and plenty of children. It was up early and bed late with him and the loom never standin' still. One mornin' his wife called to him and he busy throwin' the shuttle and she says, 'Jewel, come and ate your breakfast.'

He ignored her and went on workin' so she called again and he drove the shuttle faster than before. She tried coaxing him. 'Come at wanst, Thady dear, or your porridge will be stone cowld.'

96

'I can't, till I complate this,' said Thady.

'Faith, I'll not ax you again,' says she and she flounced off in a huff to the wash-house.

Well, he left the loom at last, and went over to the stirabout, and what would you think but when he looked at it, it was as black as a crow; for you see, it was in the height of summer, and the flies lit upon it in such a host that the stirabout was covered with them.

'Why, thin, bad luck to your impidence,' says the weaver, 'would no place sarve you but that? And is it spyling my brekquest yiz are, you dirty bastes?' And with that, bein' altogether bad tempered at the time, he lifted his hand, and he made one great slam at the dish o' stirabout, and killed no less than three score and ten flies at the one blow. It was three score and ten exactly, for he counted the little carcases one by one, and laid them out an a tin plate, for to view them.

Well, he felt a powerful spirit rising in him, when he saw the slaughter he had done, and with that, he got a swelled head, and not a stroke more work would he do that day, but out he went and was fractious and contrary to every one he met, and was squarein' up into their faces and sayin', 'Look at that fist! That's the fist that killed three score and tin at one blow – Whoop!'

With that, all the neighbours thought he was cracked, and the poor wife herself thought the same when he came home in the evenin', after spendin' every rap he had in drink, swaggerin' about the place, and looking at his brave hand every minute.

'Indeed an' your hand is very dirty, sure enough, Thady, jewel,' says the poor wife, and true for her, for he rolled into a ditch comin' home. 'You had betther wash it, darlin'.'

'How dar' you say dirty to the greatest hand in Ireland,' says he, going to strike her.

'Well, it's nat dirty,' says she, 'only a bit soiled.'

'It is throwin' away my time I have been all my life,' says he, 'livin' with you and all, and stuck to my loom, nothin' but a poor waiver, when it is Saint George or the Dhraggin I ought to be, or any one of the seven champions o' Christendom.'

'Sure what's champions to uz?' says she, 'we're paupers.'

'Don't put in your prate,' says he, 'you ignorant sthrap. You're a vulgar woman – mighty vulgar. I'll have nothin' more to say except divil a more waivin' I'll do.'

'Oh, Thady, dear, and what'll the children ate then?'

'Let them go play marvels,' says he.

'That would be but poor feedin' for them, Thady?'

'They shan't want for feedin',' says he, 'for it's a rich man I'll be soon, and a great man too.'

'Usha, but I'm glad to hear it, darlin', though I dunna how it's to be, but I think you had better go to bed, Thady.'

'Don't talk to me of any bed, but the bed o' glory, woman,' says he, lookin' mortal grand.

'Oh! God send we'll all be in glory yet,' says the wife, crossing herself; 'but go to sleep, Thady, for this present.'

'I'll sleep with the brave yit,' says he.

'Indeed an' a brave sleep will do you a power o' good my darlin',' says she.

'I'm detarmined to set off immediantly and be a knight arriant,' said he.

'A what?' says she.

'A knight arriant, woman.'

'Lord be good to me, what's that?'

'A knight arriant is a rale gintleman,' says he, 'going round the world for sport, with a sword by his side, takin' whatever he plazes – for himself. That's a knight arriant,' says he.

Well sure enough he went about among his neighbours the next day, and he got a kettle from one, and a saucepan from another, and he took himself to the tailor, who sewed him up a suit of tin clothes like any knight errant and he borrowed a pot lid, and that was his shield, and he went to a friend o' his, a painter and glazier, and made him paint on his shield in big letters –

'I'M THE MAN OF ALL MEN,
THAT KILL'D THREE SCORE AND TIN,
AT A BLOW.'

'When the people sees *that*,' says the waiver to himself, 'the sorra one will dar for to come near me.'

And with that, he told the wife to scour the small iron pot for him, 'for,' says he, 'it will make an iligant helmet;' and when it was done, he put it on his head, and his wife says, 'Oh, murther, Thady, jewel, is it

sorra one – devil of one

puttin' a great heavy iron pot an your head you are, by way iv a hat?'

'Sartinly,' says he, 'for a knight arriant should always have a weight an his brain, to keep his taughts in.'

'But, Thady, dear,' says the wife, 'there's a hole in it, and it can't keep out the weather.'

'That's fer ventiliation,' says he, puttin' it on him. 'Besides, it is aisy to stop it with a wisp of sthraw, or the like o' that if there's a downpour.'

'The three legs of it looks mighty quare, stickin' up,' says she.

'Every hemlet has a spike stickin' out o' the top of it,' says the weaver, 'and if mine has three, it's the grandher it is.'

'Well,' says the wife, getting bitther at last, 'all I can say is, it isn't the first sheep's head was dhress'd in it.'

'Your sarvint, ma'am,' says he; and off he set.

Well, he was in want of a horse, and so he went to a field hard by, where the miller's horse was grazing.

'This is the idintical horse for me,' says the weaver. 'He is used to carryin' flour and male; and what am I but the flower o' shovelry in a coat o' mail; so the horse won't be put out iv his way in the least.'

But as he was ridin' him out of the field, who should see him but the miller. 'Is it stalin' my horse you are?' says the miller.

'No,' says the weaver, 'I'm only goin' to axercise him,' says he, 'in the cool o' the evenin'; it will be good for his health.'

'Thank you kindly,' says the miller, 'but lave him where he is, and you'll obleege me.'

'I can't afford it,' says the weaver, runnin' the horse at the ditch.

'Bad luck to your impidence,' says the miller, 'you've as much tin about you as a thravellin' tinker, but you've more brass. Come back here, you vagabone,' says he.

But he was too late; away galloped the weaver and took the road to Dublin, for he thought the boldest thing he could do was to go to the King o' Dublin. He went straight to the palace and when he got into the courtyard, he let his horse loose so's he could graze about the place, for the grass was growing between the stones. The King, as it happened, was looking out of his drawing-room window and when the weaver arrived the King saw him but the weaver pretended not to notice the King and sat on the ground to rest himself after his long journey. He pretended to go to sleep but he took great care to turn out the front of his shield with the bold letters on it. The King calls to one of his courtiers.

'Look here,' says the King, 'what do you think of a vagabone like that, comin' undher my very nose to go to sleep? It is thrue I'm a good King,' says he, 'and I 'commodate the people by havin' sates for them to sit down and enjoy the raycreation and contimplation of seein' me here, lookin' out a' my drawing-room window; but that is no rayson they are to make a hotel o' the place, and come and sleep here. Who is it at all?' says the King.

'Not a one o' me knows, plaze your majesty.'

'I think he must be a furriner,' says the King, 'his dhress is outlandish.'

'And he doesn't know manners, either,' says the courtier.

'I'll go down and circumspect him myself,' says the King. 'Folly me,' says he, wavin' his hand at the same time in the most dignatious manner.

Down he went accordingly, followed by servants, and when he went over to where the weaver was lying, sure the first thing he saw was his shield with the big letters on it, and with that he brightens up. 'By dad,' says he, 'this furriner is the very man I want.'

'For what, plaze your majesty?' says the courtier.

'To kill that vagabone dragghin, to be sure,' says the King.

'Sure, do you think he could kill him,' says the courtier, 'when all the stoutest knights in the land wasn't aiquil to it, but went out in search of him and never kem back, and was ate up alive by the cruel desaiver.'

'Sure, don't you see there,' says the King, pointin' at the shield, 'that he killed three score and tin at one blow; and the man that done *that*, I think, is a match for any dragghin.'

So, with that, he went over to the weaver and shook him by the shoulder, and the weaver rubbed his eyes as if just wakened, and the King says to him, 'God save you.'

'God save you kindly,' says the weaver, pretending he didn't know who he was spaking to.

'Do you know who I am?' says the King.

'No, indeed,' says the weaver, 'you have the advantage o' me.'

102

'To be sure I have,' says the King, moighty high; 'amn't I the King o' Dublin?' says he.

The weaver fell to his knees, bowed and scraped and says he, 'I beg God's pardon and yours for the liberty I tuk; plaze your holiness, I hope you'll excuse it.'

'No offince,' says the King, 'get up, good man, and tell us what brings you here?'

'I'm in want o' work, plaze your riverence,' says the weaver.

'Well, suppose I give you work?' says the King.

'I'll be proud to sarve you, my lord,' says the weaver.

'Very well,' says the King. 'You killed three score and tin at one blow, I understan'.'

'Yis,' says the weaver. 'That was the last thrifle o' work I done, and I'm afeard my hand 'ill go out o' practice if I don't get some job to do, at wanst.'

'You shall have a job instantaneously,' says the King.

'A bucking big job,' says the weaver.

'Oh, it is not three score and tin or any fine thing like that. It is only a blaguard dhraggin that is disturbin' the counthry and ruinatin' my tenanthry wit aitin' their powlthry, and I'm lost for want for eggs,' says the King.

'Troth thin, plaze your worship,' says the weaver, 'you look as yellow as if you swallowed twelve egg yolks this minnit.'

'I want this dragghin to be moidered,' says the King. 'It will be no trouble in life to you; and I am only sorry that it isn't betther spoil for he isn't worth fearin' at all. Now I must tell you that he lives in the country of Galway in the middle of a bog, and he has an advantage over you in that.'

'Oh, I don't value it in the laste,' says the weaver, 'for the last three score and tin I killed was in a soft place.'

'When will you undhertake the job then?' says the King.

'Let me at him at wanst,' says the weaver.

'That's what I like,' says the King. 'You're the very man for my money.'

'Talkin' of money,' says the weaver, 'I'll want a thrifle o' change from you for my thravellin' charges.'

'As much as you plaze,' says the King; and with the word, he brought him into his throne room where there was an oak chest, bursting with pouches full of golden guineas.

'Take as many as you plaze,' says the King; and, sure enough, the little weaver stuffed his pockets and even stuck some down inside his vest.

'Now, I'm ready for the road,' says the weaver.

'Very well,' says the King. 'But you must have a fresh horse.'

'With all my heart,' says the weaver, who thought he might as well exchange the miller's old nag for something more elegant.

Now the weaver had no notion whatsoever of fighting the dragon, all he intended to do was line his pockets with gold, ride home on this new thorough-bred, cause a sensation in his parish and be a gentleman for the rest of his life. But the King was not as gullible as that, Kings have to be very canny or ordinary people would fool them. He put the weaver

104

on a horse that had been trained to dash straight across the centre of Ireland and to head straight for the bog in Galway where the demon dragon lived.

Four days they travelled without stopping. On the last day he saw a crowd of people running and crying 'The dragghin, the dragghin,' but he couldn't stop the horse or make him change course. He drew himself off the horse and clambered up a tree. Not a minute to spare had he, for the dragon appeared in a most imtemperate rage, and when he saw the horse he devoured it, bones and all.

Then he began to sniff about for the weaver, and at last he set his eye on him, up in the tree, and he shouted, 'You might as well come down out o' that, for I'll have you as sure as eggs is mate.'

'Divil a foot I'll go down,' says the weaver.

'Nor a care do I care,' says the dragon, 'for you're

as good as a tit-bit in my pocket this minit, for I'll lie undher this three,' says he, 'and sooner or later you must fall to my share.'

Sure enough he sat down, and began to pick his teeth with his tail, because of the heavy breakfast he made that mornin' (for he ate a whole village, prior to the horse), and he got drowsy at last and fell asleep. But before he went to sleep he wound himself all round about the tree, so that the weaver could not escape.

Well, as soon as the weaver knew he was dead asleep by the snorin' of him, he began to creep down as cautious as a fox; and he was near the bottom when a branch he was clinging to broke and down he fell, right on top of the dragon in a thud. But good luck was on his side, for where should he fall but with his two legs right across the dragon's neck. He laid hold of the beast's ears and kept his grip. The dragon couldn't bite him either because he was plonked on his back and then when he tried to shake him off our clever little weaver wouldn't stir, but clung on.

'By the hokey, this is too bad intirely,' says the dragon. 'But if you won't let go,' says he, 'by the powers o' wildfire, I'll give you a ride that 'ill astonish your siven small sinses my boy.'

With that, away he flew like a thunderbolt and where do you think he flew to? He flew straight for Dublin till he came slap up against the palace of the King. But, being blind with rage, he never saw it and he knocked his brains out – that is, the small trifling little brain he had – and down he fell stunned.

As good luck would have it, the King o' Dublin was looking out of his drawing-room window at that moment and when he saw the weaver riding on the fiery dragon (for he was blazin' like a tar-barrel) he called out to his courtiers to come and see the show.

'By the powdhers o' war, here comes the knight arriant,' says the King, 'ridin' the dhraggin that's all afire and if he gets into the palace, yiz must be ready with the fire engines for to put him out.'

But when they saw the dragon collapse outside, they all ran downstairs and scampered into the palace yard to survey the casualty at a close range. The weaver had got off the dragon's neck and running up to the King he says 'Plaze your holiness, I did not think myself worthy of killin' this facetious baste, so I brought him to yourself, for to do him the honour of decripitation by your own royal five fingers. But I tamed him first, before I allowed him the liberty for to dar' to appear in your royal prisince. You'll oblige me if you'll just make your mark with your own royal hand upon the onruly baste's neck.'

With that, the King drew out his sword and took the head off the dirty brute, as neat as if he was topping an egg. There was great rejoicing in the court now that the dragon was killed; and the King said to

the little weaver, 'You are a knight arriant as it is, and so it would be no use for to knight you over agin; but I will make you a lord.'

'Oh Lord! A lord,' says the weaver, gurgling at his own good luck.

'I will,' says the King. 'And as you are the first man I ever heer'd tell of that rode a dhraggin, you shall be called Lord Mount Dhraggin,' says he.

'And where's my estates, plaze your holiness?' says the weaver, who always had a cunning nature.

'Oh, I didn't forget that,' says the King. 'It is my royal pleasure to provide well for you, and for that rayson I make you a present of all the dhraggins in the world, and give you power over them from this out.'

'Is that all?' says the weaver, a bit snivelly.

'All?' says the King. 'Why you ongrateful little vagabone, was the like ever given to any man before?'

'I believe not, indeed,' says the weaver. 'Many thanks to your majesty . . . and long life.'

'But that is not all I'll do for you,' says the King. 'I'll give you my daughter too, in marriage.'

Now, you see, that was nothing more than what he promised the weaver in his first promise; for, by all accounts, the King's daughter was the greatest dragon ever was seen, and had the divil's own tongue, and a beard a yard long.

Lord Mount Dhraggin was quick to rebut. He thanked the King for the noblesse of his offer, but explained to him and the courtiers that he'd be riskin' bigamy and spoiling the girl's honour. They gave him a black horse as a farewell present and he rode on home to the wife more conceited than ever.

## The Swan Bride

Long ago there lived an old king in Ireland and his wife had died so he was very lonely. He had one son, Eoin, and he decided it was time for his son to marry.

'It would cheer and delight me to see you married,' the King said.

'I am willing to obey you but I know of no woman that I care for and I have never seen one that I will marry,' said the son.

Hearing that, the King decided to send for his druid.

'Tell me where my son will find the perfect bride, the one he must marry,' he asked.

'Oh, there is only one woman,' said the druid, 'who is right for your son, and she is the youngest daughter of the white-bearded Scolog. She is the wisest young

109

woman in the world and is a dazzling beauty. Of her they say:

"Skin whiter than the swan on the pool
Or the snow on the crest of the bending bough.
Her kiss is sweeter than the dew on the rose
Like the foxglove are her cheeks, like the raven her
    copious hair."

'Where does her father live and how are we to settle it?' the King asked the druid.

The druid said that he had no knowledge of where exactly the Scolog lived but that the son must walk the world until he found her.

The young man upon hearing this said that he was willing to go in search of the Scolog's daughter and he vowed that he wouldn't stop until he found her. Not long after he bid goodbye to his father and the druid and he set out and went first to the house of his foster mother and told her the whole story – how his father wanted him to be married and how the druid said that the white-bearded Scolog's daughter was the bride for him. The foster mother knew all about it because she was of the people of Dana and therefore skilled in hidden knowledge and enchantments. She said, 'I have three brothers and they live on the road that you must travel.'

She said that the eldest one knew how to find the Scolog but without the friendship of all three brothers Eoin would not be able to achieve his ambition. Then she promised him that she would give him something to gain the confidence and goodwill of her brothers. She went into the kitchen, she made three cakes of flour, and when they were baked she brought them out and she gave them to him.

'Now,' she said, 'when you come to my youngest brother's castle, he will rush at you in an endeavour to kill you and all you have to do is touch him on the breast with one of the cakes and at once he will become friendly and give you a welcome. The second and eldest brothers will also be furious at first but you can assuage them with the cakes.'

In the morning she gave him her blessing and he left carrying with him the three cakes. He travelled very fast, over hills, down into valleys, passed towns and villages and he never stopped until he came in sight of the castle. On the threshold he met a woman.

'God save you,' he said to the woman.

'God save yourself,' said she and she asked him what brought him here and whither he was going. Eoin explained that he had come to see the giant of the castle and to speak with him. The woman gasped.

'Don't be foolish ... away out of this before you meet the giant,' she said.

The King's son was adamant. He said that he had never set eyes on a giant and that he was curious to greet one. The woman predicted that his time on earth would be short but taking pity on him she brought him into the castle and gave him a glass of wine. Soon after they heard great clip-clopping as the giant arrived home.

'Fu Fo Fi Fa' shouted the giant as he entered the great hall. He was wearing a cape of sheepskins, he had a dead hog under his left arm, a dead boar under the other and he was wielding a club.

'You intruding squid,' he said.

'Sir,' said the King's son.

'I don't know whether I'll toss you in the air or squash you with my foot,' said the giant.

With that he threw his booty to the floor and went towards the young man determined to kill him, but Eoin, remembering what the foster mother told him, just touched the giant on the chest with one of the cakes. The giant beamed.

'By golly if it isn't a peace offering from my sister's son,' he said, putting an arm around the King's son.

He didn't know what to do for his visit. He ordered a feast and the best wine and the two of them ate and drank like gluttons. In fact the giant became so fond of the King's son that he insisted that they sleep in the same bed. The giant was hardly in bed before he was sound asleep and snoring like a dragon. With every breath he took he drew the King's son into his mouth and with every breath that he exhaled he drove the King's son to the rafters so that he was tossed hither and thither like a pancake and didn't get a wink of sleep. In the morning the giant made amends by giving the visitor a huge breakfast of black puddings, white puddings and haggis.

After breakfast the King's son took his leave and travelled all day with great speed and without ever stopping to rest. In the evening he came to the castle of the second giant. The welcome was gruesome. Right in front of the hall door there was a pavement of sharp razors that no man could walk on. Under the lintel of the door there were needles as big as bristles and, to make matters worse, it was a low door. The

King's son jumped over the razors and ducked in under the door. Inside he saw a woman.

'God save you,' he said.

'God save yourself,' said the woman.

The same conversation took place between them as with the woman in the first castle. This woman said that he would not be alive long and to comfort him she gave him a glass of wine. Soon they heard belching and roaring as the giant stormed in. He was a big lubbery fellow with bloodshot eyes, each one as big as a clock.

'Oh it's the pillow of death for you,' said he as he sprang at the stranger aiming a lubbery paw.

The King's son stroked him on the breast with the second cake and at once the giant was mollified and said, 'Welcome to my sister's friend from Erin.'

They had a great night of it eating and drinking and telling stories. They had fish in the shells, roasted plover and basins of blancmange. Their glasses were never empty and after a while the giant started to sing. He sang 'Kiss my Lady' and 'Jig Polthogue'. He got so hot and excited that he removed his green birredh and up popped his two big ears that were as long as if they belonged to an ass. He then did a very elaborate jig and invited his new friend to stay for a year and a day. Eoin declined and next morning, after a breakfast of salmon and cutlets washed down with lake water and strong whiskey, he set out for the castle of the third giant. Since it was beyond the sea he went in a red-skinned currach that the friendly giant had put at his disposal.

currach – a type of boat

This third castle was the most bewitching of all. It lay on a promontory above the sea shore. The roof was thatched with the down of cotton grass and the walls were as white as freshly falling snow. The hall door was made of beaten silver and when he knocked on it, dogs began to bark from inside. The third giant was playing chess and he hurled a silver chessman at Eoin which nearly pierced his brain. Eoin bravely walked towards him and with the third cake struck him on the breast. The giant blinked and then put out his hand and began a recitation in praise of visitors.

They had the choicest of viands and the best of French wines served in gold goblets and then, stretching himself on a sheepskin in front of the big fire, the giant asked Eoin to tell him why he had come. The King's son told his story from the beginning to end, and the giant said he would help him to finish his journey in safety and this was how he must do it.

'At midday, tomorrow, you will come to a lake; you are to hide in the rushes that are growing at one side of the water. Twelve swans will alight, near the rushes, and they will remove the crests from their heads and, at the same time, their swan feathers will fall from them, and they will turn into the twelve most beautiful women that you have ever set eyes on. When they go into bathe you are to take the crest of the youngest swan and tuck it into your bosom next your skin; you are to hold the other eleven crests in your hand. When the young women come out, give the eleven crests to their owners but as for the twelfth, you must tell her that you cannot give her the crest unless she carries you to her father's castle on the Island of Enchantment. She will refuse you and say she has no power and she will plead with you to give her back her crest but you must be adamant. Eventually, she will see that there is nothing for it but to grant your wishes.'

Next morning the King's son set out and travelled until he arrived at the appointed lake, and then hid himself behind the rushes. Everything happened as the giant had said and the twelve swans, upon removing their crests, turned into the twelve most beautiful white-skinned women.

When they came out of the water he took them by surprise and gave the eleven orange crests to the older ones but kept the twelfth and insisted that the young maiden carry him to her father's castle. She wept and pleaded and eventually when she put the crest on her head a strange and unexpected thing happened: she lost all her obstinancy and fell in love with the King's son. They set out for the Island of Enchantment and as they got near it she advised him what he was to do.

She said, 'Thousands of suitors and champions have come to give greeting to my father but each one of them has perished. You must stand with your right foot inside the threshold, your left foot outside and your head under the lintel. If your head is inside my father will cut it off and if it is outside he will cut it off too. You're to stand under the lintel and say the words "God save all here".'

At that the swan flew up and disappeared over a great thicket of trees. The King's son went up to the

castle door, did exactly as she had told him, and met with her father Scolog.

'You are safe,' cried the Scolog, 'but a curse upon your teacher.' Then the Scolog told a servant to bring the King's son to an adjoining building and to give him food and bedding for the night. The servant took a bundle of straw, some turf and some potatoes and put them inside the door of the building.

The King's son laid out the straw to serve as a bed and was wondering about cooking the potatoes when the swan appeared and took a small bundle from her pocket and when she opened it a silken cloth unfolded laden with the finest food and drink. He ate and he drank with relish and when he had finished the young woman whittled a little staff that turned into the finest bed that any man could lie on. She told him that her father would come in the morning to give him a test but before that he was to turn the bed over and it would shrivel into a little shaving which he could throw into the fire.

In the morning the Scolog came and this is what he said to the King's son. 'Your task is this. There is a lake on my land and a swamp at one side of it – you are to drain the lake and dry the swamp, and you are to be finished before evening; if not I will take the head from you. To drain the lake you are to dig through a neck of land two miles in width and here is the spade to do it with.'

The King's son went with the Scolog who showed him the ground and left.

'What am I to do?' said he, realising that it would need a host of men and that it would take months. For every sod he dug out, seven sods came in and soon he saw that he was getting nowhere. He threw the spade away and sat down on a heap of sods and began to cry. He wasn't long there when the Scolog's daughter came with a cloth in her hand and a small bundle.

'Why are you crying?' she said.

'My head will be off by sunset,' said he.

' 'Tis a long time from now to sunset,' said she and suddenly from the bundle she produced the most tasty breakfast.

While he was eating she took the spade, cut out one sod and threw it away. Suddenly every spadeful of earth in the neck of land followed the first spadeful; the whole neck of land was gone and soon there wasn't a drop of water in the lake or the swamp nearby. The King's son was incredulous.

In the evening the Scolog came and he was surprised to find the King's son had done such an impossible task and he was annoyed because the stranger

had got the better of him. That night the daughter
came as before and there appeared a lavish supper
and a comfortable feather bed. In the morning the
Scolog came and said, 'I have a field outside, a mile
long and a mile wide with a tall tree in the middle.
There are two wedges, an axe and a knife – you are to
cut down the tree and make from it enough barrels to
cover the whole field, then you are to fill the barrels
with water and it must be done before sundown.' The
King's son went to the field and struck the tree with
the axe but as he did the axe bounded back and hit
him in the forehead so that he was stretched flat on
the ground with a huge gash and blood pouring out
of him. He got up and tried again and the very same
thing happened so that in a short while he had three
wounds on his forehead and the life and hope was
ebbing out of him. The Scolog's daughter arrived and
spread out the cloth containing his breakfast and
while he was eating she struck one little chip from the
tree which turned into a barrel and then another
and another until the whole tree had turned into
barrels which stretched the length and breadth of
the field. Then she produced a wooden dipper and a
pail and she set the King's son to work at filling the
barrels. The moment he poured a drop of water into
a barrel it swelled up until it reached the brim.
Meanwhile the daughter was advising him about the
next eventuality.

She said, 'My father will invite you to stay in the
castle tonight but you must refuse. You must say that
you're content to lodge where you have lodged for the
last two nights.' With that she disappeared.

The Scolog came and saw that all the work had been done and he invited the King's son to his castle and was annoyed that the young man refused. As usual the daughter appeared with the supper, made a bed and told the King's son that the next day's task would be the hardest of all.

The Scolog brought the King's son to a quarry and pointed to the tools which were there – a crowbar, a pickaxe and a trowel. The King's son was to quarry all the stones and build a fine castle with outhouses, stables, cellars and kitchens. Not only that but there were to be cooks, servants in livery, dishes and utensils of every kind and priceless furnishings in every room.

The King's son began to quarry with the pickaxe and very little of the stone had been chipped away when the daughter arrived. She produced a breakfast and while he was eating she struck one stone with a little silver chisel and as she did the other stones fell away in showers and then began to form themselves into the finest and most grandiose castle. Footmen appeared, cooks in white aprons and bonnets, workmen started carrying in sideboards and mirrors and everything was set in place except for a small spot beside the fireplace. She handed the King's son a trowel and said he was to fill in the gap in front of the fireplace and wait for her father's arrival. She foretold that the Scolog would ask the King's son to his castle and that this time he must go. 'After dinner he will seat you at a table and throw red wheat on it and, as he does, three pigeons will alight on the table and start to eat the wheat. My father will ask you to choose one of his three daughters in marriage and if you wish to choose me you will recognise me by a black speck on one of my wings.'

All happened as the daughter predicted and when the King's son was told to make his choice he saw the black speck and chose the pigeon he wanted. The three jumped from the table and when they touched the floor they were three beautiful women. A priest and a clerk were called and the couple were married that night. After the festivities the King's son wanted to go home with his bride and she warned him about fresh obstacles.

She said, 'My father doesn't want to part with us . . . he will give you his blessing but that is all pretence, for he intends to follow us and kill us. You must choose a horse for the journey and you must choose the right one. He will send a man with you to three different fields; in the first field there are the finest horses but take none of them, likewise in the second; in the third there is a poor old grey nag and you are to take her because she is my mother. She has great power and my father is opposed to her and has made her into the form that she is.'

The daughter waited in hiding, inside a hollow oak tree, while the King's son selected the old grey nag. The moment he mounted her, wings sprouted from her side. He collected the daughter and she bore them both aloft, above the hills and over a range of purple-clad mountains that skirted the sea.

When the Scolog heard that the King's son had fled he turned himself into balls of red fire and set out after them. He eventually caught up with them where they had come to land on an island in the middle of

the ocean where they proposed to rest for the night. When they saw the Scolog coming the daughter uttered several conjurations which turned the mare into a boat, the King's son into a ragged fisherman, and herself into a fishing rod.

'Have you seen a man, a woman and a grey mare?' the Scolog asked of the fisherman.

'They went that way,' said the fisherman and straightaway the Scolog was zipping through the air and he never stopped till he was all around the world and back at his own castle in search of the couple. He set off again and caught up with them on the next island but the daughter had made a spinning wheel of her mother, a bundle of flax of herself and an old hag of her husband.

'Have you seen a couple and a grey mare?' asked the Scolog.

'I have,' said the old woman, 'they are fifty miles north.'

Away zipped the Scolog across the sea until he came to the shore and as he did he saw them land – his wife, his daughter and the King's son all in their natural shape. He knew then that they had deceived him and he swore he would avenge them but it was no use because his powers were invalid once they had set foot in Ireland. A chariot with four horses bore them away and they were protected by rainbows and showers of fiery dew from the slings that the Scolog hurled after them.

The old King wept on the return of his son with the beautiful bride but it was not long before his tears turned to mellow laughter as he too discovered that he had a wife for his old age.

## The White Cat

A long time ago there lived this giant called Trencross in a big stone castle surrounded by trees
and craggy rocks. The castle had twenty iron doors;
each door was guarded by a dog who had fangs thick
as iron and who was trained to tear to pieces any
interloper. Only the giant knew the private words that
would keep the dog from eating its prey and that was
why no one could pass in or out of the castle without
the giant's permission.

Now he passed his time every day going out fighting
and marauding and one day he captured the most

precious booty of all, the young beautiful Princess Cora, the orphaned daughter of a rival king. Cora was brought in a chest and laid down in this wood-panelled room with scarcely any light. She was given dwarves to wait on her and also a huge casket of jewellery so that she could change her rings and her tiara. She was demented. She refused to eat and she refused to speak. She just sat there in this dark room with her eyes closed bewailing her cruel fate.

About a week after she got there she heard a great commotion in the castle yard, the sound of horses whinnying and the bugle being blown, and she realised that the giant and his men were off on another rampage. So she thought, 'When he's gone I'm going to bribe these dwarves with jewellery and I'm going to get out of here.'

It was as if the giant could read her thoughts. In he marched in his chain-mail to tell her that he was going off on a little skirmish but that if she had any notion of escaping to please put it out of her mind because the dogs guarded every door and every window and if she tried to escape she would be torn to pieces. Then he took her hand and gave it a great, wet, slobbering kiss and he gloated over the fact that when he got back he intended to marry her. Of course she started to cry but he just laughed and said, 'Crying will spoil your beauty,' and added that he'd marry her whether she liked it or not.

The poor Princess was beside herself. She lay face down on the red sofa, and cried so much that the velvet dye reddened and stained her face. She refused food, she refused drink, and when night came she prayed that she would go to sleep and never waken up. As it happened, she wakened very early indeed; in fact before it was light. So she got up and went over to the window and looked out. The hounds were underneath guarding the castle and she thought 'I'm finished . . . I might as well be dead.'

At that moment she looked up at a big evergreen tree, saw the branches stirring and then saw a white cat come creeping along towards the window and staring at her, with a very knowing and particular look. She decided to open the window, and as she did the cat spoke to her most imperiously.

'Stand back, let me in,' said the cat.

Now the Princess was most surprised to hear a cat talking like a person, but she did as she was told and the cat gave a leap, jumped and landed in the Princess's arms.

'Who are you?' asked the Princess.

'Your friend,' said the cat.

'You mean you can help me?' said the Princess, snivelling.

'Now forget the tears,' said the cat, 'and listen to common sense. When the giant returns and asks you to marry him say that you will.'

'I won't,' said the Princess.

'Do what I tell you,' said the cat. 'When he asks you to marry him, say to him that you will, but first these dwarves must wind up three balls of dew and they must be as big as these.'

Then the cat put her paw in her fluffy bosom and took out three little crystal balls each one the size of a pea.

'Three balls of dew, do you hear.'

'But they're infinitesimal,' said the Princess.

'It will take a month to make each ball, so that gives you three months before the giant can wed you.'

At that the cat slid out of her arms and made for the window.

'Don't leave me,' said the Princess.

The cat explained that she had a rendezvous with a very important person, none other than the Prince who could rescue the Princess from the giant's clutches.

'How?' said the Princess.

'With the Milesian Sword,' said the cat. Then she instructed the Princess that she was to watch the tree each morning for the Prince's arrival and when she saw him she was to throw him the three crystal balls without speaking to him.

'If you speak, all will be lost,' said the cat and at that moment she took a leap through the window and flew through the air like a scarf. The dogs bayed but she was quite safe from them.

A few days later the giant returned and straight-away he came to the Princess's room to tell her to prepare for her wedding.

'I will wed you,' said the Princess, 'but first you must promise me something.'

'Anything you like,' said the giant, very pleased at her affability.

Cora told him how she wanted his dwarves to wind three balls of dew and she showed him the size they were to be.

'Certainly, my sweet,' said the giant, laughing at the absurdity of the request.

Nevertheless, he summoned the dwarves and ordered them to go out at dawn to gather the dew and to wind the three balls.

So the next morning the dwarves were out in the fields and searching along the hedgerows, each one gathering a tiny tiny trickle of dew. The giant was furious when after a week they had not gathered as much as a small tear and he wished that he had never made such a promise and wondered if there was some conspiracy. The Princess pretended to be very happy and even joked with him about the shortage of dew and said it was something she herself hadn't expected.

'So why did you ask?' he queried.

'A whim,' said the Princess, 'a whim.'

Now the white cat was busy setting up the rescue operation for the Princess. She had to go and find the Prince of the Silver River, a prince who was very sorrowful because he had loved Princess Cora before she was carried away. She found the Prince in his study in a right gloom, so she jumped on to his lap giving him a pat.

'I have just seen the person you are thinking of.'

'Who?' said the Prince.

'We know who,' said the cat, 'and I have come here with a plot to save her.'

She then told the Prince that Trencross the giant held Cora captive and that fierce wolfhounds guarded the doors.

'I will go there and slay the giant,' said the Prince.

'Easier said than done,' said the cat.

She told the Prince that no sword made by the

129

hands of man could kill the giant and that even if he were dead the hounds would still tear his assailant to pieces.

'So I cannot rescue her,' said the Prince.

The cat told him to sit still and listen to her orders. He was to go to the giant's castle, he was to climb the tree and tap at the window and there he would find Cora who would give him the three crystal balls which would enable him to find the famous sword that, at that moment, was kept on a special island in a brew of soporific herbs to keep it from flying. She warned him about not speaking.

The Prince set out at once and it took him two days to reach the castle. He hid in the trees and at dawn shook the branch in front of the Princess's window. Then as she opened the window he put out his hand and she dropped the three balls into it. She looked so sad that he wanted to comfort her but he remembered that he was under a bond not to. The cat was waiting for the Prince at the edge of the wood.

'Have you got the balls?' said the cat.

'I have,' said the Prince.

'Then follow me,' said the cat, and they walked and they walked until they came in sight of the sea.

When they got to the shore the cat told the Prince what to do. He was to take the red ball, he was to unravel one thread and then he was to let the ball drop into the water and pull on the single thread. As he did this he saw something ruffle the surface of the water and soon a little silver boat appeared. The cat told him that the boat would bear him to a white palace which was on a secret island where no human

had ever been. In that palace there was a famous sword and it was by this sword alone that the giant could be killed. There was also a dish with a hundred cakes and on eating these cakes the hounds would die. But there was one thing that the Prince must not do. He must not visit any other island except the one where the sword was kept. He must not eat or drink while on his quest, because if he did, he would forget all about the Princess and by then it would be too late because the giant would have married her.

'I could never forget her,' said the Prince as he

stepped on to the silver boat and floated out to sea. The days passed and the Prince went journeying on and on. At night he saw the stars and in the morning he saw the sun rise and not until the third day did he see a tiny island in the distance.

The Prince was very hungry so that when he stepped off his boat on to the island he forgot his vow and reached up and picked some guavas that were growing there wild. He did not even know what they were. At first he thought they were nuts but when he bit into one he found, to his surprise, that the flesh inside was soft and had a sweet juicy taste. He ate first out of curiosity but once he had discovered the strange taste he was ripping the shells off and eating them as fast as he could. 'They're scrumptious,' he said to himself and wondered why he had never seen them before.

The silver boat floated straight out to sea and soon the Prince forgot everything including his vow to rescue the Princess. So he wandered off into the island and after some time he heard strange sweet music like the sounds of millions of little bells and he looked and under the trees he saw three lovely maidens coming towards him and they had garlands of white flowers in their hair.

'Oh welcome, Prince of the Silver River,' said one of the maidens and then another one told him that he was most welcome and that they would bring him to the place where the King and Queen were presiding along with their beautiful daughter Eva. So the Prince allowed himself to be led along and when he saw Eva he thought her the most beautiful creature alive.

When he looked on her white skin and her long dark tresses of hair and her fevered eyes he completely forgot about Princess Cora and his other attachment.

A feast was prepared, so that he and Princess Eva could get better acquainted, and as they danced and joked and walked through the grounds picking flowers he fell deeper and deeper in love with her until at last he was lost, and like one in a trance.

Now meanwhile the dwarves were busy working away every morning on the balls of dew and they had managed to finish one ball and were halfway through another so that the Princess Cora was getting very agitated because she knew that half of her allotted time was up. Poor Princess Cora. Little did she know that even as she wept the Prince was asking for the hand of Princess Eva in marriage.

On the evening before the Prince's wedding there was a big ball arranged and the Prince was up in his bedroom getting ready. He was putting on his cufflinks and a bit absent-minded when he felt something rubbing against his leg and he looked down and what did he see but the white cat mewing up at him reproachfully. Now the minute he saw the white cat his memory came back to him. He remembered the boat, why he had set out on the journey, the promise he had made and above all the fact that Princess Cora was prisoner.

'She is still waiting for you,' said the cat in a very reproachful way.

'Oh,' he said, 'I'm sorry, but I'm getting married tomorrow.'

The cat said yes, that she was aware of this absurd

133

arrangement but that fate ordained differently. Then she said that he was to go ahead with the dance, he couldn't leave there and then, but at the first light he must creep out of that place and not let any living creature see him because if they did, he would be a prisoner for ever. When he got to the sea, he was to take the second ball, hold one of its threads, toss the rest of the ball into the sea and then by pulling on the thread he was to summon up his little magic skiff.

'I'm not sure I want to,' said he to the cat.

'I'm sure I want you to,' said the cat, disappearing.

Now at the party that night he was very distracted and in two minds about what he should do. When he looked at the Princess Eva he felt very tempted as she was looking very beautiful in a blue dress with net over it and sequins in her gold hair.

'Tell me you are happy,' she said, as they waltzed.

'I am happy,' he said but his heart was not in it. He knew then that he would have to go and that some power stronger than his own was invisibly at work. He knew a bond had been placed upon him and his mind was made up before the dance had ended.

He was up long before the cocks crowed and hurried out of the palace with a sack over his head. Nevertheless, a guard must have spotted him because just as he neared the shore he heard screaming in the woods and hissing voices calling his name. It was the Princess and her ladies-in-waiting who were chasing him, and though he was tempted to look back, he didn't.

As he threw the ball, a glistening boat bobbed up; he stepped on to it, took his place in the prow, and soon the boat was scudding over the water like a seagull.

Three days and three nights passed and still he had not come to the next island. He feared that maybe he would have to float about for ever. He had almost given up hope when, in the distance, he saw a green strip of land and as the boat glided in he saw that the island was dotted with small trees and that the trees were laden with blood-red berries. They were very tempting but he remembered that he must not eat. Then something happened to weaken his resolve. As he docked the boat, a branch trailed above his head and the berries were literally falling down his face in front of his lips and in an impulse, and without even thinking of what he was doing, he ate some and having tasted them he found they were delicious so he lay down on his boat and gorged himself.

Later on he decided to investigate and he walked through the forest; as he was walking he heard a great guffawing and he saw a bevy of giants coming towards him. One giant caught him by the waist and just picked him up as if he were a matchstick.

'Who are you, you little squid?' said the giant.

'I am the Prince of the Silver River,' said the Prince.

'Ho-ho,' said the giant, 'and what brave deeds has the Silver Prince done?'

'None yet,' said the Prince and he dimly remembered that there was something he should do. The giantess stepped forward and tweaked his cheek and said she knew what he would be good for, that he would be delicious to eat. She said his white skin would broil very tenderly indeed and she proposed having him for supper. The other giants laughed and said there would be not enough of him to go around.

'In that case we'll have to fatten him up,' said the giantess putting her great arm around him and leading him home.

In her kitchen she stuffed him with food and when he said he couldn't eat any more she just held him in front of a huge fire and asked him how he would feel about being burnt alive.

The Prince was watched day and night and was force-fed for most of his waking hours, while at the same time the Princess was sitting in her castle looking out at the evergreen tree, despairing.

The giantess decided that the Prince was fat enough and indeed he was like a roly poly so she came to him and told him that he had only one more day to live but true to their giantly custom he could have a wish. Naturally, the Prince wished for his life to be saved.

'Don't be ridiculous,' she said. 'We haven't fed you up for nothing.'

And the Prince said in that case he had nothing else he wanted to wish for. Well, he spent the last hours out of doors in the courtyard and never was there a sadder Prince. He could hear the comings and goings in the kitchen and the cooks discussing how they would cook him and wondering how many hours he would take and wondering what sauces and condiments to serve with him and who should have the choicest parts of him and so forth.

'I want the crackling, I want the crackling,' he heard an impudent young giant say.

From behind a big urn he spotted the white cat peeping out. Now the minute he saw the white cat he again remembered the silver boat, his journeys across the sea, the red berries that had almost forced themselves into his lips, and his broken vow.

'Oh, thank God you're here,' said the Prince.

'It is not for your sake,' said the cat because she was livid with him.

She said he deserved to be eaten and that she would never have come to rescue him only that Princess Cora was in sore need of him. She railed against the fact that he was the only one who could rescue the Princess. The Prince hung his head when he heard the name Princess Cora and he asked what had befallen her.

'Her time is nearly up,' said the cat, and explained that the third ball of dew would be wound before two days.

Then she said that she had come to give him a last chance. She told him that he was to go to the giantess and say that in fact he now had a wish and the wish was to go down and look at the sea for the last time, but of course when he went down to the sea he was

to throw out his third ball, summon up the silver ball,
summon up the silver boat and hop into it and travel
like billyo.

The giantess was in two minds about his request.
For one thing she didn't see the sense of it and for
another she sniffed about, and wondered if there was
any conspiracy.

'I love the sea and the memory of it will console me
when I am being roasted,' said the Prince.

She decided to grant his request and asked one of
her servants to please have it printed on a tablet as an
example of her clemency.

The Prince went down to the sea, unwound the third
ball and was way out in the ocean before any of the
giants came on his trail. Again the boat skimmed the

waves and as night fell the Prince sat at the helm but with an utter sense of desolation because he knew that he had so little time left. He sailed all night and just before dawn he found himself by an island where there was a little strip of biscuit-coloured sand. This time he was more resolved. He jumped ashore and set out. The palace was in the centre of the island and to his great surprise it was guarded by white chinchilla cats. They nodded as if they were expecting him and inside he saw that the great hall was filled with cats but some were at the table eating cakes and pastries while others were frisking and jumping about the room playing with coloured balls. In the middle of the room there was a marble pillar with a mother of pearl throne and he reckoned that this was reserved for the King or the Queen of cats.

His white cat appeared wearing a crown and in full regalia. She was hoisted up on to the throne by her attendants. She looked at him a little haughtily.

'Do you know me?' she said.

'Oh I do,' said the Prince, 'but I didn't know you were royal.'

He curtsied and then she asked if he would like something to eat.

'No thank you,' said the Prince remembering his orders and at this she seemed very pleased. She told her servants to fetch the sword and the hundred cakes.

The sword was brought in a big copper pan which was covered over with rushes. The sword itself rested in a brew of soporific herbs; it had to be kept there as otherwise it would leap up of its own accord and engage in battle. 'Oh, my Destiny,' exclaimed the Prince when he saw it. It was so gleaming that it looked as if it were on fire.

The cat told him not to be frightened but to pick it up, and as he picked it up an enormous strength came on to him and he was certain that he heard the sword humming.

She then placed in his hand a beautiful brooch and said it was her wedding present to the Princess. The Prince set off for the shore followed by all the cats and when they saw him step on to his boat they let out meows of good luck. The boat bobbed over the water like a will-o'-the-wisp and travelled at an almighty speed and the Prince was back in the giant's wood before dawn. When the hounds saw the Prince coming up the drive they bounded towards him leaping and snarling and were intent on tearing him to pieces but as they sprang to his throat the Prince threw the cakes at them and as each hound devoured a mouthful it staggered and fell dead.

Then the Prince arrived at the front of the castle and in a loud clear voice he summoned the giant to come out and fight with him. Immediately doors and windows were flung open, more hounds bounded out only to be sated with the poisonous bread and eventually the giant himself came out in his wedding regalia. Now he was furious because in fact it was his wedding day and he did not want to be challenged to a fight. The giant took great umbrage and he said, 'Neither fell nor flesh of thine shall escape this day.'

With that they started up upon the courtyard and they attacked one another and struck at one another, the giant with his club and the Prince with his sword, and so fierce were they and so deft that all the onlookers could see was the clash of the point of the weapons and the contestants leaping in the air, at times like salmon and then crouching like moles, and swinging from left to right as they stunned one another with the breath feat, the apple feat, the ghost feat, the screw feat, the cat feat, the red whirling feat, the barbed feat, the wheel feat and then worst of all the dragon feat, and so on they struggled and wrestled and tore into one another so that the poor Prince's body was black with blood and his skin was bruised and there were welts on his thighs and even the giant was black and purple with his tongue lolling out.

When it grew dark the servants had to bring out the torch flames and the giant's face looked more treacherous than ever before. They fought on and on until the gong sounded saying that it was dinner time and the giant suddenly announced that they had fought enough, that they would quit and begin on the morrow. Hearing this the Prince lay down his sword and just as he did the giant came up at him from the rear, caught him unawares and levelled a blow at him with his club knocking him almost to the ground. Despite the force of the blow the Prince had enough presence of mind to pick up the sword and renew the fight.

Anger came on him then and the hero light shone about him and he plucked up all the strength that was inside him and it was as if the sword itself had turned into a thinking weapon. There commenced then a merciless attack on the giant, the sword piercing him deeply in the centre of his chest and hacking right through his huge stomach so that he bled and called for his aides. The strange thing was that no one came to his rescue.

Soon he was staggering, his shield in front of his belly to keep his entrails from falling out. He shouted for a tub of marrow to heal his wounds but it was too late – he fell in a heap on the cobbled ground, cursing his household.

'Trencross is dead. Trencross is dead!'

The words echoed through the courtyard but were not followed by any cries of lament because Trencross was feared by all. Only his dog began to moan for him. The Princess had stayed in her room all the time but now the battle was over the dwarves and the others shouted her name and when she leaned out of

the window they cheered wildly. Looking up, the
Prince wondered how he could have forgotten such
an exquisite and faithful creature and there and then,
in front of all the guardsmen, he opened his heart to
her.

'Will you forgive me?' he begged.

'There is nothing to forgive,' said the Princess and
at that two men stood on the shoulders of two other
men and reached up to the window and lifted her out,
and laid her carefully on a dais so that the Prince
could propose to her formally.

The cat attended their wedding, looking quite splendid in her tiara and her white ermine cloak and the
Prince drank a special toast to her as 'keeper of true
love'.

## Gilly

Gilly Blackfoot was so named because he was always getting into mischief, falling into puddles and hardly ever bothering to wash himself. Near the farm where he lived there was a fort of big trees and it was so dark in there that you would need a torch to light the way, even in broad daylight. People said that fairies congregated there on certain nights when the doors between the two worlds are flung open and spirits come up from the nether world to make merry or to steal some person of worth.

On Halloween Gilly decided to creep out of bed and go down to the fort to see if he would come across any of these fairies. It was so cold that the dogs didn't even bother to follow him, they let out a yelp or two and went back to sleep. As Gilly walked down the path towards the fort of trees he thought he heard some chattering but decided it was probably due to his imagination but then as he got nearer he heard a sound as of silver bells all tinkling together, an orchestra so soft and so melodious that it filled the night. There before his eyes was a whole troop of fairies dressed in the most lavish costumes and up to all sorts of pranks. They were just as Gilly had heard them described, a few inches in height, wearing green caps with cocky feathers and very impudent in their ways. Some were dancing, some were drinking from little crystal goblets which were about the size of a thimble and others were playing tig in and around the fort and making a terrible racket. The fort itself was lit with little magic gold tapers and even the leaf mould looked very beautiful. There were he-fairies and she-fairies and they seemed to be saying some chant which Gilly could not understand because they all spoke so fast. He began to lose his nerve and was about to run back when up comes a marshal fairy, taps him with a baton on the knee and says 'Hello Gilly Blackfoot.'

'Hello,' said Gilly trying to be nonchalant. His legs were like jelly and his breath sounded like a penny whistle inside him.

'Would you like a joy ride?' said the marshal.

'I can't,' said Gilly.

'Ah, you distasteful little squid,' said the second fairy who stood in front of him with gritted teeth. All around, Gilly could hear the other fairies saying it was time to go and all of a sudden he felt his two hands pulled behind his back and a chant in his ear 'Roolya-Boolya, Roolya-Boolya, Roolya-Boolya, Roolya-Boolya.' In the distance there was the thunder of hooves and at once a whole host of riderless horses came over the field. They were jet black horses with black manes and silver harnesses and they lay down on the ground so that the fairies could mount them.

> 'By Yarrow and Rue
> And my red cap too
> Hie over to England.'

They were chanting this as Gilly found himself thrown on a big high horse and a rein put in his hands. There was a very joking fairy on the horse next to him and as they set out he shouted 'jump to it nuncle.' Gilly found himself soaring up into the air surrounded by horses on all sides and loud chanting.

> 'By Jonquil and chance
> By wild horses' prance
> We'll hie us to France.'

It was all at a terrific speed, so much so that Gilly didn't dare look down, but from the chanting going on around him he knew that they had crossed the Irish Sea and were going towards Dover, bound for France.

When they landed in France he was pulled from his horse and the fairies formed a dense huddle around him. It was then he learned their wicked plot which was to carry off a princess; and he, Gilly, was essential

to them because it was on his horse she would ride,
since a fairy cannot sit beside a mortal. Her name was
Irma and the password was 'Get Irma'. They were in
the grounds of the palace where she lived. In the
moonlight Gilly could see that it was made of stone
and ramparts and turrets all about. There was an owl
hooting. No one could see Gilly or his companions
because the chief fairy had made them invisible; they
were aerial beings.

'Roolya-Boolya, Roolya-Boolya,' they chanted as
they advanced towards the door, passing the guard
dogs who did not even sniff them. A great feast was
going on inside. All the noble men and noble women
of the land had gathered there because the King was

about to give his daughter Irma in marriage, to a Prince from Syria. When Gilly caught sight of the Princess he gasped. She was very young and was splendidly dressed with her bright yellow hair bound by circlet of gold and she was wearing shoes with silver embroidery on her small white feet. She had a lace mantle that was fastened in front by a diamond brooch and underneath, next to her soft snow-white skin, was a garment of white brocade. Everything about her was beautiful except for her eyes that looked like misted pearls so sad were they. Her father the King was leading her up the aisle of the church where bishops waited to marry her. She looked from left to right as if she wanted to escape and Gilly, knowing what lay ahead for her, pitied her with all his heart. He and the fairies were advancing up the aisle, covered in a mist that lay like a net over them.

From the opposite wing of the church the groom appeared, followed by a retinue. He was fat and very flashily dressed and he wore a gold cap that stuck up like a drum on the top of his head. The jesting fairy told Gilly how unhappy the Princess was at having to marry Prince Podge but that her father insisted on it because the Prince had vast riches in Syria.

All of a sudden, as the bride and the King were advancing to the strains of organ music, there was the most terrible commotion and confusion. Three of the lead fairies stepped before the bride and put their batons out while other fairies formed rings around, and as the Princess took the next step she fell forward on to her face and before she could rise or be picked up they had thrown a net over her head and uttered words that made her invisible. The King was jumping up and down in an apoplexy and his crown was jumping up and down with him as he shouted out 'Irma, Irma, Irma.' The bishops were looking very startled and the whole congregation was in an uproar as Gilly heard a fairy tell him to pick Irma up and run for the door. He had no choice but to pick up this creature who seemed lifeless and was light as a feather, and he hurried down the aisle with sentinels of fairies guarding him on either side. As he got to the garden he heard the same wild sounds 'Roolya-Boolya, Roolya-Boolya' and just as before the horses appeared fully caparisoned and ready to fly. As they rose into the sky Gilly heard, from behind him, his passenger crying and begging to know where she was being brought. He would have liked to comfort her but he couldn't and he did not dare tell her the truth. The first words that he spoke to her was when they had landed in Ireland and he was helping her down.

'May God protect you,' said Gilly and as he said it the most amazing thing happened. The horses turned into handles of ploughs and bits of broken sticks and the fairies began to hiss and fume at him like a pack of weasels.

'You traitor,' said the marshal fairy because as soon as God's name was mentioned the Princess was protected and could not be carried away. Cries of rage and fury arose on every side; Gilly was hemmed in with curses and thumps and each fairy thinking up the most terrible punishment for him. There is no knowing what they would have done to Gilly except that it was the hour of morning when they had to vanish underground and the bugle

was blowing, summoning them to the Underworld.
'Vamoose . . . Vamoose,' the marshal called. They
disappeared like specks of dandelion seed, just drifting
away out of sight. Three elder fairies whispered to one
another and then one of them, who was very old and

hunched, came forward and struck the Princess a slap upon the face so that she staggered and fell. He laughed as he did it.

'She won't be able to say a word, she's a dummy now,' he told Gilly and added that they would get

151

even with him for ruining their plot. Then they all disappeared and silence fell on the fort and on the fields around and for the first time Gilly breathed freely. But when he looked at the poor Princess lying there he became desperate. He picked her up and there she stood in her wedding dress thin and shivery, her skin showing through her clothes, white as snow. He could not tell whether she'd heard him or not when he spoke because the expression on her face did not change. It was one of woe and perplexity. Gilly took off his jacket and put it around her as he pondered on what to do. He did not want to bring her back to France immediately because the marriage would go ahead and anyhow he had no horses or no transport. He thought and he thought and he decided that he would bring her to his godmother who lived in a big house on a great estate.

When they got to his godmother's house she received them very kindly and put Irma sitting by the fire with a rug over her knees. She resolved with Gilly that they would keep the girl safely and send a letter to the King of France to say that she was safe. She said that sometimes merchants came to sell her tapestries or vessels, and that these merchants always travelled back through France to the East. But for the time being they decided they would tell no one about Irma. Poor Irma sat there with her head down, giving no response at all so that they did not even know if she understood or appreciated what they said. The godmother then spoke to her in French and to these remarks too she remained dumb and indifferent.

Now the months wore on and Irma began to be a

little more cheerful. She helped in the garden, she embroidered some cushions, she sometimes smiled when Gilly and the woman addressed her, but she never spoke and she never appeared to understand. Letters were sent by two merchants but no reply came and Gilly could only assume that they got lost or else that her father wanted nothing more to do with her, realising that she'd been carried away by a fairy tribe who put her under an enchantment. He decided that there was only one thing for it which was to wait for the fairies to come again and to put himself at their mercy, or maybe to learn some secret by bribing one of them. The next time that they were due for one of those midnight forays he waited at the fort, with a torch in one hand and his father's ash plant in the other. He decided that he was going to be very brave but he did not feel at all brave as he looked in the distance and heard the strange soft melodious sound that presaged their arrival. They were the same fairies as before and they sprung up around him like myriads of mushrooms, wearing their green caps with the jaunty feathers and shrieking joyously, 'Roolya-Boolya, Roolya-Boolya.'

'Oh, you're here, said the hunchback who had struck the Princess down. As the horses galloped over the fields throwing up clods of earth behind them, Gilly wondered if perhaps he shouldn't go back to France and go straight to the King and tell him everything that had happened but then it occurred to him that the fairies were probably going to Spain or to Germany to filch another princess since they had lost out on their previous guest.

'Ah you distasteful traitor,' said one of them as

Gilly ventured to ask a question, indeed to ask for help.

'No matter,' said the hunchback, 'he can't converse with the girl, he can't court her.'

This time they were not waiting to have any drinking or any frolic, they were leaping on to their horses and soaring into the air. To his great amazement Gilly found the jester fairy lagging behind, and just before he mounted he whispered in Gilly's ear, 'Cry to it, nuncle, give her the herb that grows in your garden.'

'Which one?' said Gilly, but the jester was way up over the trees and off.

'And boil it, nuncle,' he shouted.

Now Gilly was more agitated than ever, not knowing which herb it could be, but he resolved that he would look at every herb and every weed that grew in their garden and he would boil every single one and examine their properties. He could not sleep a wink that night; he left the curtains open and he rose with the first sign of light. He took a carving knife and headed straight for the kitchen garden and there, as he started near one wall, he saw thistles, ferns, dock leaf, hips and haws, convolvulus, masses of things that he'd seen all his life, and then under a bush he saw this odd little plant that seemed to sparkle, seemed to speak to him. Its little silver hairs seemed to be humming and the leaves made a zing-zing. He pulled up a stalk, broke it and as he did a white sap-like milk oozed out. Then he pulled another and another and he decided that this must be what the jester fairy had talked about.

Near the kitchen garden there was a boiler house so he went across, kindled the fire and put the broken bits of stalk into a saucepan to boil. Now it occurred to him that maybe the stuff was poison and that the fairy was playing a trick on him so that the Princess would die and on that account he knew that he had to taste the stuff first. He was very fearful. As he put it to his lips he wondered if maybe he should not abandon the whole idea, throw the stuff away and leave the Princess to her unhappy fate.

'But you love her,' he heard himself say. Yes, he

loved her. He had not realised it before, but he knew now that when he called on her every day, when he saw he sitting in the garden or helping in the kitchen he was totally in love with her and fearful that she would go away. Having her there even as a dumb person was far better than not having her at all. The liquid did not taste too bad and he drank several gulps of it but did not remain awake to judge its effect. Before minutes had passed Gilly had fallen into a deep sleep in which he had a beautiful dream – Irma and he walked out of a gigantic wedding cake and went up the aisle of a church. He came to, with some hens clucking around him, and a crick in his neck. Not only that, but he was speaking French, he was making a speech, thanking the lords and ladies at his wedding reception.

'It works, it works,' said Gilly as he hurried off to his godmother's house with the saucepan of brew.

The drink had made him much more confident. He told them how he had waited for the fairies, how he had got the hint from the jester, how he had tried the brew himself and how no harm had come to him – indeed he felt stronger. The girl drank willingly, and as she did, she fell back on to a *chaise longue* and sank into a profound slumber. Gilly and his godmother watched and waited all day and when Gilly touched her and she did not even stir he was worried that maybe she had drunk too much. Sometimes he leaned in and whispered something to her in French but she was lifeless like some statue from which came the faintest and most serene breath. Eventually, her foot stirred and they saw her raise her arms above her head and give a little yawn followed by a most beautiful smile. She wakened and looked at them both but made no effort to speak. Gilly and his godmother were in terrible suspense, torn between hope and despair as they ventured a question. They asked her if she had slept well.

'Very well, thank you,' she said, in the most beautiful lilting voice. Gilly, insane with joy, asked her to speak again, in God's name, to say a lot of things so that they would know that the power of speech was hers. The Princess sat up and said that the first thing she must do was to thank them both for the kindness and forbearance they had shown to her, adding that she hoped to repay their hospitality by inviting them to France.

'You mean you'll leave us,' said Gilly dreading the prospect of having to live without her ever again.

'We will go together, you and I, and our guardian here, and we will ask my father to relieve me of the promise of marriage and let me be betrothed . . .'

'To who?' said Gilly.

'To you, my sweet,' said the Princess as she put her dainty hand out and asked him to kiss it in the French manner. Gilly was not sure if he knew the protocol but at any rate he knelt and delivered a ceremonious kiss so that she laughed and asked if he had been schooling himself in French customs over the months.

'*Oui?*' she asked saucily.

Now it was Gilly's turn to be struck dumb. Such a change had come over her: her cheeks flushed as if cochineal had been poured on them, her eyes shone like wet opals and she tripped about exclaiming how *heureuse* she was, and announced when they were married they would divide their time between Ireland and France, and live in pink stone castles, with woods and waterfalls all around.

'Speak, *mon poulin . . .*' she teased, but Gilly could not speak; he was tongue-tied, being too full of love and adoration for her.

## Paddy the Piper

'It was in the time of the 'ruction, whin the long summer days was cut short by raison of the martial law – that wouldn't let a dacent boy be out in the evenin', good or bad; for whin the day's work was over, divil a one of uz dar go to meet a frind, or a girl at the dance, but must go home, and shut ourselves up, and never budge, nor rise latch, nor dhraw boult, antil the morning kem again.

''Twas afther nightfall, and we wor sittin' round the fire, and the praties wor boilin', and the noggins of butthermilk was standin' ready for our suppers, whin a nock kem to the door.

praties – potatoes

'"Whisht!" says my father, "here's the sojers come upon us now," says he; "bad luck to thim, the villains, I'm afeerd they seen a glimmer of the fire through the crack in the door," says he.

'"No," says my mother, "for I'm afther hangin' an owld sack and my new petticoat agin it, a while ago."

'"Well, whisht, any how," says my father, "for there's a knock agin;" and we all held our tongues till another thump kem to the door.

'"Oh, it's a folly to purtind any more," says my father, "they're too cute to be put off that a-way. Go, Shamus," says he to me, "and see who's in it."

'"How can I see who's in it in the dark?" says I.

'"Well," says he, "light the candle thin, and see who's in it, but don't open the door, for your life, barrin' they brake it in," says he, "exceptin' to the sojers."

'So with that I wint to the door, and there was another knock.

'"Who's there?" says I.

'"It's me," says he.

'"Who are you?" says I.

'"A frind," says he.

'"Baithershin," says I, "who are you at all?"

'"Arrah! don't you know me?" says he.

'"Divil a taste," says I.

'"Sure I'm Paddy the Piper," says he.

'"Oh, thunder an turf," says I, "is it you, Paddy, that's in it?"

'"Sorra one else," says he.

'"And what brought you at this hour?" says I.

sorra – devil of one else (no one else)

161

'"By gar," says he, "I didn't like goin' roun' by the road," says he, "and so I kem the short cut, and that's what delayed me."

'"Oh, murther!" says I, "Paddy, you know yourself it's a hangin' matther to be cotched out these times."

'"Sure I know that," says he, "and that's what I kem to you for," says he; "so let me in for owld acquaintance sake," says poor Paddy.

'"Oh, by this and that," says I, "I darn't open the door for the wide world; and sure you know it; and troth, if the Yeomen ketches you," says I, "they'll murther you, as sure as your name's Paddy."

'"Many thanks to you," says he, "for your good intintions; but plase the pigs, I hope it's not the likes o' that is in store for me, anyhow."

'"Faix then," says I, "you had bettheer lose no time in hidin' yourself," says I; "for, throth I tell you, it's a short trial and a long rope the Yeos would be afther givin' you – for they've no justice, and less mercy, the villains!"

'"Faith thin, more's the raison you should let me in, Shamus," says poor Paddy.

'"It's a folly to talk," says I, "I darn't open the door."

'"Oh then, millia murther!" says Paddy. "What'll become of me at all at all?" says he.

'"Go aff into the shed," says I, "behin' the house, where the cow is, and there there's an iligant bed o' straw, that you may sleep in," says I.

'So off Paddy set to hide in the shed, and throth it wint to our hearts to refuse him, and turn him away from the door, more by token when the praties was ready – for sure the bit and the sup is always welkim to the poor thraveller. Well, we all wint to bed, and Paddy hid himself in the cow-house; and now I must tell you how it was with Paddy.

'You see, afther sleeping for some time, Paddy wakened up, thinkin' it was mornin', but it wasn't mornin' at all, but only the light o' the moon that desaved him; but at all evints, he wanted to be stirrin' airly, bekase he was goin' off to the town hard by, it bein' fair day, to pick up a few ha'pence with his pipes – for the divil a betther piper was in all the counthry round, nor Paddy; and every one gave it up to Paddy that he was iligant an the pipes, and played "Jinny bang'd the Weaver" beyant tellin', and the "Hare in the Corn" that you'd think the very dogs was in it, and the horsemen ridin' like mad.

'Well, as I was sayin', he set off to go to the fair, and he wint meandherin' along through the fields, but he didn't go far, antil climbin' up through a hedge, when he was comin' out at t'other side, his head kem plump agin somethin' that made the fire flash out iv his eyes. So with that he looks up – and what do you think it was, Lord be marciful to uz, but a corpse hangin' out of a branch of a three.

'"Oh, the top o' the mornin' to you, sir," says Paddy, "and is that the way with you, my poor fellow? Throth you tuk a start out o' me," says poor Paddy; and 'twas thrue for him, for it would make the heart of a stouter man nor Paddy jump, to see the like, and to think of a Chrishthan crathur being hanged up, all as one as a dog.

'Now, 'twas the rebels that hanged this chap –

bekase, you see, the corpse had good clothes an him, and that's the raison that one might know it was the rebels — by raison that the Husshians and the Orange-men never hanged any body wid *good* clothes an him, but only the poor and definceless crathurs, like us. So, as I said before, Paddy knew well it was the *boys* that done it; "and," says Paddy, eyin' the corpse, "by my sowl, thin, but you have a beautiful pair o' boots an you," says he, "and it's what I'm thinkin' you won't have any great use for thim no more; and sure it's a shame for the likes o' me," says he, "the best piper in the sivin counties, to be trampin' wid a pair of owld brogues not worth three traneens, and a corpse with such an iligant pair o' boots, that wants some one to wear thim."

'So, with that, Paddy lays hould of him by the boots, and began a pullin' at thim, but they wor mighty stiff; and whether it was by raison of their bein' so tight, or the branch of the three a-jiggin' up and down an not lettin' Paddy cotch any right hoult o' thim — he could get no advantage o' thim at all, and at last he gev it up, and was goin' away, whin lookin' behind him agin, the sight of the iligant fine boots was too much for him, and he turned back, determined to have the boots, anyhow, by fair means or foul. And I'm loath to tell you how he got thim, for indeed it was a dirty turn, and throth it was the only dirty turn I ever knew Paddy to be guilty av. And you see it was this a-way: 'pon my sowl, he pulled out a big knife, and, by the same token, it was a knife with

traneens — wisps of straw

a fine buck-handle, and a murtherin' big blade, that an uncle o' mine, that was a gardener at the lord's, made Paddy a prisint av; and, more, by token, it was not the first michief that knife done, for it cut love between thim, that was the best of frinds before; and sure 'twas the wondher of every one, that two knowledgeable men, that ought to know betther, would do the likes, and give and take sharp steel in frindship; but I'm forgettin' . . . Well, he outs with his knife, and what does he do, but he cuts off the legs of the corpse; "and," says he, "I can take off the boots at my convaynience." And throth it was, as I said before, a dirty turn.

'Well, sir, he tuck'd the legs undher his arms, and at that minit the moon peeped out from behind a cloud. "Oh? Is it here you are?" says he to the moon, for he was an impidint chap – and thin, seein' that he made a mistake, and that the moonlight deceaved him, and that it wasn't the early dawn, as he conceaved; and bein' freken'd for fear himself might be thrated like the poor corpse he was afther a malthreating, if *he* was found walking the counthry at that time – by gar, he turned about, and walked back agin to the cow-house, and, hidin' the corpse's legs in the sthraw, Paddy wint to sleep agin. But what do you think? Paddy was not long there antil the sojers came in airnest, and, by the powers, they carried off Paddy – and faith it was only sarvin' him right for what he done to the poor corpse.

'Well, whin the mornin' kem, my father says to me, "Go, Shamus," says he, "to the shed, and bid poor

thrated – treated

Paddy to come in, and take share o' the praties, for, I go bail, he's ready for his breakquest by this, any how.''

'Well, out I wint to the cow-house, and called out "Paddy!" and afther callin' three or four times, and gettin' no answer, I wint in, and called agin, and dickins an answer I got still. "Tatthar-an-agers!" says I, "Paddy, where are you at all at all?" and so, castin' my eyes about the shed, I seen two feet sticking out from undher the hape o' straw. "Musha! thin," says I, "bad luck to you, Paddy, but you're fond of a warm corner, and maybe you haven't made yourself as snug as a flay in a blanket? But I'll disturb your dhrames, I'm thinkin'," says I, and with that I laid hould of his heels (as I thought, God help me), and givin' a good pull to waken him, as I intinded, away I wint, head over heels, and my brains was a'most knocked out agin the wall.

'Well, whin I recovered myself, there I was, an the broad o' my back, and two things stickin' out o' my hands like a pair o' Husshian's horse-pist'ls – and I thought the sight 'd lave my eyes, when I seen they wor two mortial legs.

'My jew'l, I threw them down like a hot pratie, and jumpin' up, I roared out millia murther. "Oh, you murtherin' villain," says I, shakin' my fist at the cow, "Oh you unnath'ral baste," says I, "you've ate poor Paddy, you thievin' cannible, you're worse than a neygar," says I; "and bad luck to you, how dainty you are, that nothin' 'id sarve you for your supper, but the best piper in Ireland. Weirasthru! Weirasthru! What'll the whole counthry say to such an unnath'ral murther? And you lookin' as innocent there as a lamb,

and atin' your hay as quiet as if nothin' happened."
With that, I run out – for, throth, I didn't like to be
near her – and, goin' into the house, I told them all
about it.

'"Arrah! be aisy," says my father.

'"Bad luck to the lie I tell you," says I.

'"Is it ate Paddy?" says they.

'"Divil a doubt of it," says I.

'"Are you sure, Shamus?" says my mother.

'"I wish I was as sure of a new pair o' brogues," says I.
"Bad luck to the bit she has left iv him but his two legs."

'"And do you tell me she ate the pipes too?" says
my father.

'"By gor, I b'lieve so," says I.

'"Oh, the divil fly away wid her," says he, "what a
cruel taste she has for music!"

'"Arrah!' says my mother. "Don't be cursin' the
cow, that gives the milk to the childher."

'"Yis, I will," says my father, "why shouldn't I
curse sich an unnath'ral baste?"

'"You oughtn't to curse any livin' thing that's
undher your roof," says my mother.

'"By my sowl, thin," says my father, "she shan't be
undher my roof any more; for I'll sind her to the fair
this minit," says he, "and sell her for whatever she'll
bring. Go aff," says he, "Shamus, the minit you've ate
your breakquest, and dhrive her to the fair."

'"Throth I don't like to dhrive her," says I.

'"Arrah, don't be makin' a gommagh of yourself,"
says he.

gommagh – a fool

'"Faith, I don't," says I.

'"Well, like or no like," says he, "you must dhrive her."

'"Sure, father," says I, "you could take more care iv her yourself."

'"That's mighty good," says he, "to keep a dog, and bark myself," – and, faith, I rec'llected the sayin' from that hour – "let me have no more words about it," says he, "but be aff wid you."

169

'So, aff I wint – and it's no lie I'm tellin', whin I say it was sore agin my will I had anything to do with sich a villain of a baste. But, howsomever, I cut a brave long wattle, that I might dhrive the man-ater iv a thief, as she was without bein' near her, at all at all.

'Well, away we went along the road, and a mighty throng it wuz wid the boys and girls – and, in short, all sorts, rich and poor, high and low, crowdin' to the fair.

'"God save you," says one to me.

'"God save you kindly," says I.

'"That's a fine baste you're dhriven'," says he.

'"Throth she is," says I, though it wint agin my heart to say a good word for the likes of her.

'"It's to the fair you're goin', I suppose," says he, "with the baste?" (He was a snug-lookin' farmer, ridin' a purty little gray hack.)

'"Faith, thin you're right enough," says I, "it is to the fair I'm goin'."

'"What do you expec' for her?" says he.

'"Faith, thin, mysel doesn't know," says I – and that was thrue enough, you see, bekase I was bewildhered, like, about the baste entirely.

'"That's a quare way to be goin' to market," says he, "and not to know what you expec' for your baste."

'"Och," says I, not likin' to let him suspect there was anything wrong wid her. "Och," says I, in a careless sort of a way, "sure no one can tell what a baste 'll bring, antil they come to the fair," says I, "and see what price is goin'."

'"Indeed, that's nath'ral enough," says he. "But if you wor bid a fair price before you come to the fair, sure you might as well take it," says he.

'"Oh, I've no objection in life," says I.

'"Well, thin, what 'ill you ax for her?" says he.

'"Why, thin, I wouldn't like to be onraysonable," says I (for the thruth was, you know, I wanted to get rid of her), "and so I'll take four pounds for her," says I, "and no less."

'"No less!" says he.

'"Why, sure that's chape enough," says I.

'"Throth it is," says he, "and I'm thinking it's too chape, it is," says he, "for if there wasn't somethin' the matter, it's not for that you'd be sellin' the fine milch cow, as she is to all appearance."

'"Indeed thin," says I, "upon my conscience, she is a fine milch cow."

'"Maybe," says he, "she's gone off her milk, in regard that she doesn't feed well?"

'"Och, by this and that," says I, "in regard of feedin' there's not the likes of her in Ireland; so make your mind aisy – and if you like her for the money, you may have her."

'"Why, indeed, I'm not in a hurry," says he, "and I'll wait to see how they go at the fair."

'"With all my heart," says I, purtendin' to be no ways consarned – but in throth I began to be afeard that the people was seein' somethin' unnath'ral about her, and that we'd never get rid of her, at all at all. At last we kem to the fair, and a great sight o' people was in it – throth, you'd think the whole world was there, let alone the standins o' gingerbread and iligant ribbins, and makins o' beautiful gownds, and pitch-and-toss, and merry-go-rouns, and tints with the best

av dhrink in thim, and the fiddles playin' up t'incourage the boys and girls. But I never minded thim at all, but detarmint to sell the thievin' rogue av a cow afore I'd mind any divarshin in life. So, an I dhriv her into the thick av the fair, whin all of a suddint, as I kem to the door av a tint, up sthruck the pipes to the tun av "Tather-Jack-Welsh" and my jew'l, in a minit the cow cock'd her ears and was makin' a dart at the tint.

'"Oh, murther!" says I, to the boys standin' by, "hould her," says I, "hould her – she ate one piper already, the vagabone, and, bad luck to her, she wants another now."

'"Is it a cow for to ate a piper?" says one o' thim.

'"Not a word o' lie in it, for I seen his corpse

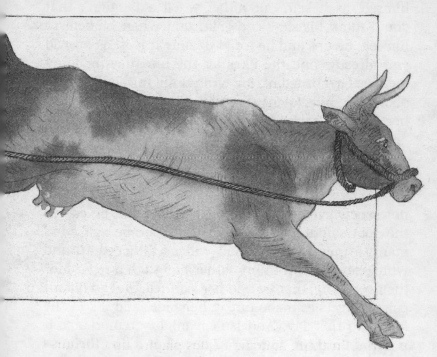

myself, and nothin' left but the two legs," says I; "and it's a folly to be sthrivin' to hide it, for I *see* she'll never lave it aff – as Poor Paddy Grogan knows to his cost, Lord be merciful to him."

'"Who's that takin' my name in vain?" says a voice in the crowd; and with that, shovin' the throng a one side, who should I see but Paddy Grogan, to all appearance.

'"Oh, hould him too," says I. "Keep him av me, for it's not himself at all, but his ghost," says I, "for he was kilt last night to my sartin knowlodge, every inch of him, all to his legs."

'Well, sir, with that, Paddy – for it *was* Paddy

himself, as it kem out afther – fell a laughin', that you'd think his sides 'ud split; and when he kem to himself, he ups and he tould uz how it was, as I towld you already; and the likes av the fun they made av me was beyant tellin', for wrongfully misdoubtin' the poor cow, and layin' the blame av atin' a piper an her. So we all wint into the tint to have it explained, and by gor it took a full gallon o' sper'ts t'explain it; and we dhrank health and long long life to Paddy and the cow, and Paddy played that day beyant all tellin', and many a one said the likes was never heerd before nor sence, even from Paddy himself – and av coorse the poor slandhered cow was dhruv home agin, and many a quiet day she had wid us afther that; and whin she died, throth my father had sitch a regard for the poor thing, that he had her skinned, and an iligant pair of breeches made out iv her hide, and it's in the family to this day. And isn't it mighty remarkable it is, what I'm goin' to tell you now, but it's as thrue as I'm here, that from that day out, any one that has thim breeches an, the minit a pair o' pipes sthrikes up, they can't rest, but goes jiggin' and jiggin' in their sate, and never stops as long as the pipes are playin' – and there,' said he, slapping the garment in question that covered his sinewy limb, with a spank of his brawny hand that might have startled nerves more tender than mine, 'there, them is the very breeches that's an me now, and a fine pair they are this minit.'